THE LIFE RECOVERY® WORKBOOK FOR

Sexual Integrity

A Bible-Centered Approach for Taking Your Life Back

STEPHEN ARTERBURN & DAVID STOOP

Tyndale House Publishers
Carol Stream, Illinois

Visit Tyndale online at www.tyndale.com.

TYNDALE, Tyndale's quill logo, and Life Recovery are registered trademarks of Tyndale House Publishers.

The Big Book is a registered trademark of A.A. World Services, Inc.

The Life Recovery Workbook for Sexual Integrity: A Bible-Centered Approach for Taking Your Life Back

Copyright © 2020 by Stephen Arterburn and David Stoop. All rights reserved.

Cover photograph of orange abstract copyright © pox.na.vse.mail.ru/Depositphotos.com. All rights reserved.

Cover design by Dan Farrell

Edited by Ellen Richard Vosburg

The author is represented by the literary agency of Alive Literary Agency, 7680 Goddard Street, Suite 200, Colorado Springs, CO 80920, www.aliveliterary.com.

Unless otherwise indicated, all Scripture quotations are taken from the Holy Bible, New Living Translation, copyright © 1996, 2004, 2015 by Tyndale House Foundation. Used by permission of Tyndale House Publishers, Carol Stream, Illinois 60188. All rights reserved.

The brief excerpts from Alcoholics Anonymous and the Twelve Steps are reprinted and adapted with permission of Alcoholics Anonymous World Services, Inc. Permission to reprint and adapt the Twelve Steps does not mean that AAWS has reviewed or approved the contents of this publication, or that AAWS necessarily agrees with the views expressed herein. A.A. is a program of recovery from alcoholism only—use of the Twelve Steps in connection with programs and activities which are patterned after A.A., but which address other problems, or in any other non-A.A. context, does not imply otherwise. Additionally, while A.A. is a spiritual program, A.A. is not a religious program. Thus, A.A. is not affiliated or allied with any sect, denomination, or specific religious belief.

The profiles in this workbook are composite characteristics of persons who have had the courage to work the steps on various issues in their lives and on their own addictive behaviors. Names, ages, and situations have been modified to protect their anonymity.

For information about special discounts for bulk purchases, please contact Tyndale House Publishers at csresponse@tyndale.com, or call 1-800-323-9400.

ISBN 978-1-4964-4212-3

Printed in the United States of America

26 25 24 23 22 21 20
7   6   5   4   3   2   1

This workbook is dedicated to every fellow struggler who has had the courage to face the truth about themselves, the humility to abandon their flawed attempts at living, and the willingness to find God's truth and live accordingly.

CONTENTS

The Twelve Steps

1. We admitted that we were powerless over our problems and that our lives had become unmanageable.
2. We came to believe that a Power greater than ourselves could restore us to sanity.
3. We made a decision to turn our wills and our lives over to the care of God.
4. We made a searching and fearless moral inventory of ourselves.
5. We admitted to God, to ourselves, and to another human being the exact nature of our wrongs.
6. We were entirely ready to have God remove these defects of character.
7. We humbly asked God to remove our shortcomings.
8. We made a list of all persons we had harmed and became willing to make amends to them all.
9. We made direct amends to such people wherever possible, except when to do so would injure them or others.
10. We continued to take personal inventory, and when we were wrong, promptly admitted it.
11. We sought through prayer and meditation to improve our conscious contact with God, praying only for knowledge of his will for us and the power to carry it out.
12. Having had a spiritual awakening as a result of these steps, we tried to carry this message to others, and to practice these principles in all our affairs.

The Twelve Steps used in *The Life Recovery Workbook* have been adapted with permission from the Twelve Steps of Alcoholics Anonymous.

INTRODUCTION

If you keep yourself pure . . . your life will be clean, and you will be ready for the Master to use you for every good work. (2 Timothy 2:21)

This workbook is about transformation from death to life, from sexual addiction to recovery. It's about walking humbly, righteously, and mercifully with God while accepting his will. In our compulsions and addictions, we have opposed God's will by hurting ourselves, our bodies, and our loved ones. We have been separated from God and from other people. The Twelve Steps are a path to finding that humble walk that leads us out of self-centeredness and closer to God's heart.

We will be examining the Twelve Steps individually to consider the challenging spiritual lessons that allow us to live free of bondage every day. Each step has a new task for us, but none of the steps is meant to stand alone. For successful recovery, they are meant to be worked in order. Each step prepares us for the next one, as we develop a greater sense of openness to God's plan and purpose in our lives.

Although the path of recovery involves hard and sometimes painful work, it is worth the effort. God will meet us on this path as we become willing to take each step toward new life. We see the Twelve Steps as a path and a process that makes us better disciples and more committed followers of Jesus Christ. Honesty, humility, and courage are vital components of faith that can move us beyond our sexual addictions to a vibrant way of living as a follower of Jesus. Welcome to the journey.

STARTING AND LEADING A GROUP

Recovery is best experienced in the context of a group. Two or more willing people can form a powerful bond as they study and work these steps together. With little effort on your part, your struggles, problems, and hang-ups become a blessing to the group. As you open up, everyone else will feel more free to share from their own lives.

Being the leader of a group is actually quite simple. You can find many books on how to lead a small group, but here's a simple and effective way to do it:

1. Find a location in your home, a church, a workplace, or school, and obtain permission (if necessary) to form the group.
2. Put up a few flyers announcing the time and place, calling it a support group for sexual addictions, recovery group, or Twelve Step group.
3. Show up early, arrange the chairs, make some coffee, and welcome people as they arrive.
4. Start when you say you will start by opening in prayer and by reading the Twelve Steps and the correlating Scriptures.
5. Ask if anyone would like to share for three or four minutes. Don't allow others to "fix" the speaker, and if he or she goes on too long, be sure to enforce the time limit.
6. Make sure everyone has a copy of the workbook. Ask them to study Step One for discussion at the next meeting.
7. End when you say you will end by reading the Lord's Prayer.
8. Be sure that everyone knows where to get a workbook and a *Life Recovery Bible*, if they don't already have one.
9. E-mail us—Stephen Arterburn at sarterburn@newlife.com; David Stoop at drstoop@cox.net—and tell us how it's going.
10. Feel good that you are allowing God to use you.

Please remember that working the steps is an art, not a formula. Most often, it is an individualized process.

God be with you on this journey. We pray that you will find healing, serenity, and peace of mind.

PROFILE

Shame can drive your life to the point of unmanageability. It drove Daniel's life to the point of unmanageability and nearly committing suicide at the worst phase of his sexual addiction. No one knew he had a problem except for his wife (Carol), me, and possibly the Federal Bureau of Investigation. I would have never known about it, if not for a phone call from Carol that changed everything. Carol did not know Daniel was a sex addict. She did not know the extent of his problem. She just knew what he revealed to her, with his car keys in his hands, just before he was going to drive out into the country and kill himself. His gun was already in the car.

As his addiction had progressed, one of his greatest fears and the source of his enormous shame was Carol finding out. Part of Daniel's problem was his idealization of Carol, and he did not think someone so "good" could ever accept someone as "bad" as him. He had assumed that if she ever did find out, or if he ever came clean and confessed his double life to her, she would leave him immediately and tell the world what he was really like. His world was quite large, as he was one of the most respected Bible teachers in the evangelical Christian community.

There were times he came close to telling her, but then he would back down. When the FBI seemed to be about to enter the picture, he immediately shut down, sank into a deep depression and started to obsess over how he would kill himself. He settled on the gun-in-the-middle-of-nowhere scenario as the best choice. He thought the headline would be all about his great life, his struggle with depression, and his sad ending. His plan was to drive across a bridge over a very large lake and toss his phone and laptop out the window to sink all of the evidence. Once his plan was in place, the only detail he couldn't control or manage was the FBI. His confusion and desperation led him to tell Carol the truth before he drove away. He screwed up the courage to tell her, rather than have people in suits show up at the door and shock her with the horrible truth.

When Daniel told Carol why he had been so distraught and what his double life had been like, he was the one that was shocked. Rather than scream or throw things or insult him, Carol teared up and embraced him; they held each other and cried for a very long time. Her first words were of love, compassion, care, and sorrow for him and all he had been struggling with for so long by himself. Rather than put more shame on him, she requested that he hand her his phone and allow her to call me (Steve) for help.

I had not talked to Daniel in over a decade, but his information was still in my contacts and I answered the call with a smile. But it wasn't Daniel calling, and my smile faded quickly. Carol was weeping and difficult to understand. Within a few minutes I understood perfectly what was going on and why she sounded so desperate. She told me about throwing out the one small sliver of hope in the form of her request to call me. I affirmed her for getting him help before she allowed all of the natural reactions to come pouring out. When she handed the phone back to Daniel, he told me how his life had become unmanageable due to his addiction and how he had reached the point of powerlessness, desperation, and suicide.

It was difficult for Daniel to talk, but he did not ask Carol to leave. He told me the story of how his addiction began when he was young and spiraled out of control as he grew older. Daniel had been exposed to pornography by his older brother when he was only seven years old, and it eventually became a daily habit. He thought his problem would end when he married Carol, but it didn't. Over the years, he increasingly sought out more extreme forms of pornography until he finally found himself seeking out child pornography.

When Daniel clicked onto the child porn site and started to look at the images, they shocked him. The real shock came when a message appeared on the screen displaying the FBI seal and claiming to know who he was, where he lived, and that he would be contacted by personnel from the FBI. It was that message that awakened Daniel to what he had been doing, how far it had gone, and how much shame was within him.

Daniel saw no way out but suicide. He was still acting on his own to control his life. He was still trying to manage things. It was quite fortunate that in a moment of confusion—or rather, a divine intervention—he confessed to his wife, and she responded in love rather than reacting in anger. That phone call put Daniel on a different trajectory that has led him to over a decade of victory for himself and a satisfying marriage for the two of them.

Daniel went to an Every Man's Battle intensive weekend with New Life, and that was where he was able to admit his powerlessness over the problem and see the complete and total unmanageability of his situation for the first time. His life had been out of control and unmanageable for years, but like so many of us, it takes a crisis to change our course and then find a path to hope and healing. The crisis for Daniel seemed like the worst thing that could happen to him, but the crisis was the gift that led him to take a look at the first of the Twelve Steps of Life Recovery.

STEP ONE

We admitted that we were powerless over our problems and that our lives had become unmanageable.

The recovery journey begins when we confront the very first word in Step One: *we*. This immediately challenges the isolationist in us. Although we would be more comfortable with the word *I* and would prefer to get better alone, only *we* can recover. The Twelve Step program guides us into community, where all involved are a part of each other's recovery. The Twelve Steps are worked and lived in a group; independence is deadly for any addict. Spiritual transformation always begins in community. When Jesus began his ministry, he created a group. When we look at the church in the book of Acts, we find groups meeting in homes. Living in open and honest community is necessary for spiritual growth—we have to accept help from others in order to recover from whatever addiction or codependency issues we have.

We admitted we were powerless. Admitting that something or someone is more powerful than our own will confronts our pride. So we keep on acting out with unhealthy sexual behaviors born out of our dependency and addiction, and we continue to attempt to control it. By attending meetings and listening to other people's stories, we become more open to the possibility of recovery. Our pride must be shattered, a little at a time, because we will not recover without an admission of powerlessness. Our very human nature rebels at the idea of powerlessness, which signifies our inability to escape our life of dependency and addiction on our own strength. We must let go of image seeking and pride and tell the truth about our demoralized condition.

Step One contains a potent paradox: By telling the truth about our complete powerlessness over addiction, we receive the power of choice in return. To jump into recovery waters with both feet, we must go even deeper. Not only must we admit and accept our powerlessness over our dependencies and addiction, but we must also concede that our lives are unmanageable. This strikes a second blow to our pride and self-sufficiency. We have continued in the delusion that there should be something we can do on our own, especially to clean up our own lives. However, addiction leads to inefficiency in our jobs, to dissatisfaction in our relationships, and quite often, to a sense that life is not worth living.

Our emotional pain underscores the reality of our inability to manage our lives. Our loner mentality must give way to joining the "we" of recovery. We have to be rid of the "just Jesus and me" belief system that leads to more isolation and shame. When we realize that even God is in community (Father, Son, and Holy Spirit), we become aware of the fact that human beings were created to be connected to others.

The meditations for Step One include some examples from Scripture of people struggling with powerlessness. Naaman had position and power in the military that blinded him to his powerlessness (see 2 Kings 5:1-15). He began to demand things from life, thinking that he was special because of his position. We may do this as well, both at work and at home. We may have an inflated sense of importance because of our ministry. We may demand things from our families or coworkers based on our way. Like Naaman, we will find that this type of pride that resists input and direction from others leads to isolation. Only God can deal with this rebellion in our hearts. The consequences of addiction are sometimes the only way by which God can break through to us.

Sometimes we arrive at powerlessness and unmanageability by losing everything, as Job did (see Job 6:2-13). Being in recovery and trying to walk a spiritual path does not mean that we will be spared our share of snags and obstacles. In these times, recovery can appear to be hopeless and not worth the work. The rebel in us that wants control will counsel, "This is just too hard. Your troubles must mean that God doesn't like you." At this point, we need a group of people to continue pointing us to God no matter what happens. We need people who will nurture hope even in the most difficult places. As we hit bottom and face our powerlessness over all of life, we need encouragers. We need to be reminded of Jesus' saying that "if you try to hang on to your life, you will lose it. But if you give up your life for my sake, you will save it" (Luke 9:24). This is another way of describing powerlessness.

By exploring our powerlessness, we will have to confront and oppose negative ideas that tell us that being powerless means being a victim. By coming to the end of our own power, we develop enough humility to hear the voice of God and do his will.

The apostle Paul—before his conversion and transformation, when he was still known as Saul—could not explore powerlessness at all. He was intoxicated by the power he wielded, even if it placed him in opposition to God's plan for his life. Yet, God pursued Saul, despite his power-hungry, murderous state of mind, to call him to a new direction, a totally transformed purpose. So that he could stop persecuting the gospel and start preaching it, God made him totally blind and dependent on others to lead, feed, and shelter him. He had to accept powerlessness and unmanageability in order to be used by God in powerful and amazing ways.

We must also first accept our powerlessness and inability to manage before we can be freed from addiction and become a channel for God in ways we could never imagine. We are so schooled in the thought that we can do anything we put our minds to that it is almost impossible to envision the power of God in us, doing what we have not been able to do to this point. God in us, shining through human vessels, gives us the ability to recover, to accept powerlessness, and to accept unmanageability. We are then opened to a life powered by God rather than by our dependencies, our addictions, or our fallible selves.

When God's power lives in us, we can be pressed by troubles, perplexed by life, and haunted by our addictions or dependencies, and at the same time experience peace in trouble, hope in perplexing situations, and a lifting of the compulsion to act out. When we admit our powerlessness, God's power flows in to fill us and accomplish what we could never do on our own.

QUESTIONS FOR **STEP ONE**

No-Win Situations *Genesis 16:1-15*

1. What feelings do I have toward people in my life who are in the position of power (such as a supervisor, spouse, religious leader, or sponsor)?

_____

_____

_____

2. Who is the person from my childhood who is most likely tied to this reaction?

_____

_____

_____

3. What do I try to escape from? What do I feel trapped by?

_____

_____

_____

4. How do I use sex to escape my feelings, such as anger, boredom, fatigue, insecurity, or loneliness?

_____

_____

_____

5. When things are out of control or when I am in a no-win situation, what is my reaction (to relationships, work, promotions, kids who question or rebel, daily frustrations, financial difficulties, people who hurt or disappoint me, or God, who seems to be silent)?

_____

_____

_____

6. If I could, how would I change my response?

_____

_____

_____

Dangerous Self-Deception _Judges 16:1-31_

1. What is the longest time I have been able to stop acting out sexually?

_____

_____

_____

2. What are some of the lies and excuses I tell myself when I start acting out again?

_____

_____

_____

3. What are the things I think I can control? How do I lie to myself and about what?

_____

_____

_____

4. What is so scary about telling the truth?

_____

_____

_____

5. As I explore powerlessness, what blind spots have I discovered?

_____

_____

_____

6. How has pride affected my recovery process?

_____

_____

_____

_____

A Humble Beginning _2 Kings 5:1-15_

1. What are the differences between humiliation and humility in my life?

_____

_____

_____

2. How do I regard myself as being a little more important than other people?

_____

_____

_____

3. What makes me think I am in control of my sexual addiction?

_____

_____

_____

4. How do I keep God at arm's length and disregard those who follow him?

_____

_____

_____

5. When have I placed unrealistic expectations on other people or God?

_____

_____

_____

6. When have my attitudes shown that I believe I know better than God?

_____

_____

_____

7. Why is it difficult for me to follow instructions?

_____

_____

_____

Hope amid Suffering Job 6:2-13

1. What kind of people do I hang around with and trust? Are they people who criticize or people who encourage truth? Why do I choose to be around people like that?

_____

_____

_____

2. What emotions and behaviors do I associate with my hitting bottom?

_____

_____

_____

3. What have I done in the past to deal with pain, sadness, and loneliness?

_____

_____

_____

Like Little Children Mark 10:13-16

1. What happened to me in the past that provokes this behavior in me today?

_____

_____

_____

2. When do I feel the most cared for?

_____

_____

_____

3. What do I see in my life that reveals God's care for me?

_____

_____

_____

4. How could I replace sexual encounters with true caring and intimacy?

_____

_____

_____

A Time to Choose _Acts 9:1-9_

1. When I continue to pursue my own agenda without asking God for direction, what happens in my life?

_____

_____

_____

2. Are there areas of my life in which God may have to use extreme measures before I will listen for direction? Which areas in the past? Which areas today?

_____

_____

_____

3. What will it take for me to listen to God?

_____

_____

_____

The Paradox of Powerlessness _2 Corinthians 4:7-10_

1. Describe some instances in which you have demonstrated acceptance of your own powerlessness and God's powerfulness.

_____

_____

_____

2. How do I respond when I am in trouble?

_____

_____

_____

3. How do I respond to change?

_____

_____

_____

4. What do I do when it seems that God or someone else has abandoned me?

_____

_____

_____

5. How has trying to control my sexual impulses and desires on my own made my life more unmanageable?

_____

_____

_____

Prayer for Step One

Dear God,
Help me to be open to who you are and what you have for my life.
Help me to forget about who I thought you were and find you as
you really are.
Amen.

PROFILE

The stigma and shame related to struggling with sexual sin have always seemed much greater for men than for women. But women also struggle with sexual sins, like lust, extramarital affairs, and other related issues. Until a few years back, most people thought that pornography was only appealing to men because women are not as visually stimulated as men but instead prefer romance, touch, and nurture. For years sexual addiction seemed like an exclusively male problem.

With all that in mind, we at New Life were a bit shocked when we opened the doors to treat sexual addiction, and many women came to us for help. How Rachael came to be there was even more surprising.

Rachael was brought up in the church by a faithful Christian family that assumed she would follow their teachings and adhere to their values. That assumption—along with having a preoccupied mother—led to her being on her own when it came to dealing with sexual temptation as a teenager. Because Rachael felt disconnected from her family, almost all of her relational and emotional intimacy came from the men she dated or encountered. It was not long until every relationship became sexual.

When Rachael felt sad and depressed, she sought out a man to lift her mood. When she had something good happen, such as a promotion, a raise, or recognition, she did not go out and celebrate with female friends: It was always a date with a man that she wanted. Men were medication, and sex was her favorite drug. By the time she was thirty, she was realizing that sex was something different for her than it was for her friends. She read articles in her favorite magazines about romance addiction or relationship and sexual addiction. She knew she was a sex addict, but it took an astounding tragedy for her to want to change.

One evening at a bar she met a man who acted like he was not married but obviously was. They chatted casually, but it seemed that they both knew where they were headed that night. It was the first of many sexual encounters that happened in a variety of locations. The man was a pilot and owned a small airplane that was hangared nearby. As every sex addict knows, sexual experiences have diminishing returns, and the addiction drives toward greater risks and intensity. Rachael went up with her pilot friend on her first non-commercial flight, and she loved it. Especially "messing around" while flying. It became a weekly ritual that they both managed their schedules around until the routine was interrupted by conscience.

Rachael told the staff at New Life that at first, she thought it was just some new feelings of shame that rose up from what her church taught her as a child. Then she realized that it was something different. It was much more like a direction forward than an old inner criticism from her past. The message was two-fold: The first part was a crystal clear self-diagnosis that she had a problem with addiction and she needed help. The second part was that she was not to go up in the plane that weekend with her partner. It felt like a message from God. She called the pilot and canceled their weekend plans and ended their relationship.

Rachael's pilot friend went anyway, and it was his last flight. Just off the coast of Long Beach, California, the small plane he was flying crashed into the ocean and sank. No one survived. When Rachael learned of the crash, she was stunned. She made an appointment with a therapist to figure out what to do with her life and what to do about her problem.

Her therapist happened to be a Christian who had attended the open house of our treatment program in Anaheim. With little hesitation, she suggested Rachael check herself into our program for the treatment of sexual addiction. She did, and it was on the next Sunday morning at a chapel service that Rachael came to a glaring realization. She realized that her life was out of control, and she was not able to help make it better on her own. She had gone against everything she had been taught was right and wrong. She had betrayed herself, she had betrayed at least one other woman, and if it were not for some supernatural warning, she would be dead. She came to believe that morning in chapel that the warning was from a Power greater than herself that she knew was God. And on that morning, she also came to believe that the God who warned her was also the God who wanted to help her take her life back and restore the sanity that sexual addiction had taken from her.

STEP TWO

We came to believe that a Power greater than ourselves could restore us to sanity.

As we have faced our powerlessness to stop the deadly progression of addiction in Step One, we have admitted our complete defeat. Because there is no hope available within ourselves (our sinful, human condition), Step Two describes the process by which we look outside ourselves to develop hope that there is a Power that can stop the addictive process.

This step begins with recognizing that addiction produces a season of insanity. What usually begins innocently as seeking pleasure, relief, or comfort becomes, over time, a coping mechanism for avoiding reality and responsibility. The pain of dealing with the upsets, hardships, and disappointments of life can wear down our faith and confidence in God. Acting out sexually and other addictive behaviors can be a way of managing our stress and our sense of being out of control. As time goes on, unfortunately, these coping mechanisms turn against us. Instead of relief and comfort, we find more difficulties and troubles. We multiply our problems instead of solving them.

When we face the fact that we have been, in a sense, insane to think that we could make life work by acting out in our addiction, we see that our belief in God and in his Son, Jesus, has been nullified. Our faith has been overthrown by our addictive thoughts and behaviors and choices, and we are headed toward spiritual disaster. Surrendering the reins of our lives is not easy. We have to face our arrogant thinking and realize that although we believe in God, we have not allowed him into our lives in a real and practical way. We have not fully understood how desperate we are for his restoration and healing. When we can honestly accept that we are not God, and that he must have more room in our lives than we have previously given him, we will come closer to releasing our arrogance. We have been trying to bend life to our will and have not considered God's will at all.

In the meditations on this step, we look at Scriptures that describe what happens when we try to live in our own power. First, we begin to think that God is unfair; we begin to question him and wonder if he is really with us, as Job did. Our "insanity" in this case is in having the arrogance to think that we could actually see the whole picture as God does, and know what is fair or unfair. Coming to believe for Job meant accepting that he was a finite human, and that God is omniscient (see Job 14:1-6).

We may become grandiose like Nebuchadnezzar and think that we have the right to declare how life should revolve around us, our needs, and our wishes. This king looked at his successes and began to claim the credit for himself. He lost the humility of remembering that God rules and gives power and success "to anyone he chooses" (Daniel 4:32). His grandiosity of thought and attitude was revealed in a dream that he had Daniel interpret. Daniel pleaded with him to turn from his sin of grandiose thinking, but his ego was hooked by the pride of accomplishment: "By my own mighty power, I have built this beautiful city as my royal residence to display my majestic splendor" (Daniel 4:30).

God did not allow Nebuchadnezzar to continue in that way; he was humbled by God with a season of insanity and grazed aimlessly with the cattle in the fields until he acknowledged God's power and sovereignty. This king's grandiose thinking is similar to the grandiosity of addiction—we try to make life work by medicating, avoiding, or filling ourselves with more and more sex, food, relationships, or substances. What eventually happens is similar to what happened to Nebuchadnezzar: We end up wandering aimlessly, humiliated, and not accomplishing much. His season of insanity was like our season of addiction.

After his pointless drifting, this king came to his senses by looking up to heaven and acknowledging that life did not revolve around him, but around God. In the same way, to be relieved of addiction, we realize that our way of dealing with life has not worked. Our years of medicating our emotions with substances or compulsive behaviors have not brought the sense of comfort we were seeking. As we face the insanity of choosing to cope with life in these ways, we look up to heaven to find the all-powerful God.

Addiction is also a type of insanity in the way that it affects our internal world. Jesus came upon a man who had so many demons inside him that they were called Legion. Addiction is like that—we become consumed with demons of envy, jealousy, fear, and hate that drive us away from relationships and toward the tombs of isolation, bitterness, and hopelessness. We need Jesus to drive out these demons and restore us to our right minds, put us back on our feet, and heal our hearts, as he did for this man.

If our addiction goes on for years, we can become outcasts

from society. We might feel like the woman in the Gospels with the issue of blood, who was cut off from society by her status as unclean. Our addiction cuts us off from relationships, and we are unable to find acceptance from people. Isolation and loneliness are terribly painful, and they are not what God intended for us. It is essential for us to restore our relationships and connections with people if we are to emerge from our addictions and make a successful recovery. Our insanity must be healed by our reaching out for God as the unclean woman did. She hesitantly and feebly sought Jesus in the crowd, thinking, "If I can just touch his robe, I will be healed." Reaching out to others is a tangible sign that we are reaching out for God's healing in our lives.

Once we can face and accept that we have been insane in these ways, we are closer to recognizing how desperately we need God's touch to restore us. Coming to believe in Step Two is a process of becoming aware of a greater reality than anything we can see with our eyes. God is willing at any moment to help us overcome our addictive behaviors and unmanageable emotions. By engaging in this process, we allow God to restore us to right thinking and to clear faith in his power. Then we can be free from the isolation, the grandiosity, and the tortured thoughts and feelings that accompany addiction.

QUESTIONS FOR **STEP TWO**

Persistent Seeking *Job 14:1-6*

1. How has life seemed unfair to me in areas of family? Was there trauma and abuse? Was there a lack of teaching about sex?

_____

_____

_____

2. What are my objections to trusting God fully with my sexual desires and behaviors?

_____

_____

_____

3. What emotions, questions, and confessions do I need to be honest with God about?

_____

_____

_____

4. Am I willing to work through the pain and unfairness of my sexual addiction in order to find God and be free from this? What holds me back?

_____

_____

_____

Grandiose Thinking _Daniel 4:19-33_

1. When in my addiction, in what ways did I display the belief that I was only accountable to myself?

_____

_____

_____

2. How have I tried to use sex to have power over the events, outcomes, and people in my life?

_____

_____

_____

3. In what ways did I show that I forgot that God is ultimately in control?

_____

_____

_____

4. How have I avoided acceptance of God's power over my life?

_____

_____

_____

Internal Bondage *Mark 5:1-13*

1. What self-destructive behaviors have I inflicted on myself due to my sexual addiction? List and describe them.

_____

_____

_____

2. How has my sexual shame kept me from living my life? How has it allowed me to be more comfortable in "tombs" of isolation, anger/rage, or silent judgment?

_____

_____

_____

3. Have I begun to make excuses and accept that I am being trapped in my addiction? Am I ready to invite Jesus to visit me in my "tombs" and cleanse me? If so, write out a prayer to him here:

_____

_____

_____

Healing Faith *Luke 8:43-48*

1. How have I tried to control my problems using sex?

_____

_____

_____

2. What were the results? How did it make me feel afterwards?

_____

_____

_____

3. Is there any other way that I would like to try to control and manage it?

_____

_____

_____

4. Am I ready to do my part, as this woman courageously did, by reaching out for recovery in faith that Jesus' power will be there? Write out a statement of readiness to God.

_____

_____

_____

Restoration *Luke 15:11-24*

1. How has my sex addiction led me to compromise my values, convictions, and principles?

_____

_____

_____

2. How have my compulsions with sex dehumanized me and brought me shame?

_____

_____

_____

3. In light of my addiction and dependency on sexual relationships, how has it degraded me?

_____

_____

_____

4. Am I now open to a deeper level of believing that the power and forgiveness of God will restore me to sanity?

_____

_____

_____

Come to Believe _Romans 1:18-20_

1. How have my experiences shown me that my way of living is not a satisfying, productive, or healthy way to live?

_____

_____

_____

2. How have I seen God's power at work in other people's lives?

_____

_____

_____

3. What are the signs that I am on the path and in the process of being restored to sanity?

_____

_____

_____

Prayer for Step Two

Lord,
Help me to see the futility of trying harder and harder to control my problem and control my life each day. Help me feel your love and experience your power. Draw me closer to you so I can fully trust you with all that I am and all that I do.
Amen.

PROFILE

Robert grew up in a faithless home. Both of his parents were respected scholars, and while they remained primarily focused on their careers rather than their children, they did pass along to Robert a care for the world, a good sense of humor, and a disbelief in religion, especially Christianity. One experience in Robert's childhood had a profound impact on the rest of his life: At the age of twelve, Robert was taken advantage of sexually by a seventeen-year-old girl.

As a child, Robert loved theater. From age eight on, he was in at least two plays a year. When he was twelve, the local high school choir director selected him to play the part of Oliver Twist in the musical production of *Oliver!* One of the female students befriended Robert and his parents, and after a few rehearsals, they trusted her to bring Robert home after rehearsal. Robert instantly developed a huge crush on her. He did not believe he was too young to be in love. Because he was so smart for his age, he felt like an equal to her in their conversations. The first time she dropped him off, it seemed only natural when she reached over to give him a goodbye hug. The hugs got longer with each drop-off, and pretty soon all he could think about was how wonderful that hug made him feel.

After a couple of weeks, they stopped going straight home and began to detour to secluded locations. Soon their conversations turned into kissing and other kinds of intimate touching.

Before the musical was finished, those encounters became
sexual. As the final production of the musical came closer, she
talked to him about how wonderful their times together had
been but that they could no longer have contact with each
other after it was over. He understood it, accepted it, and when
his role as Oliver was finished, he was sad and set out to find
someone his own age who could provide relief for the way
he felt.

It was not long until Robert was in a relationship with a girl
his age. He was energized in her presence and very quickly
their relationship became sexual. There was no intercourse in this
relationship nor any of the others until he was older, but every
relationship became sexual quickly. It was the only way he felt
connected and accepted. He thought he was just like everyone
else, but for him, the sexual intimacy became a form of survival.

After college Robert married Jessica, whom he met in gradu-
ate school where they both earned doctorates. They taught at the
same university, and soon they had published their own books.
Being scholars and authors came with promotional and speaking
events when they were not teaching. So they were frequently separated when they were on school breaks. It was not long before
the opportunity came for Robert to be alone with a woman who
found him fascinating. And just like his first forbidden encounter, she made the first move, and he willingly responded. That
illicit encounter led to hundreds of other encounters with other
women over a ten-year period. As sex became less and less frequent at home, the sex away from home increased dramatically.
Soon it was an addiction that Robert could not stop.

Robert did not want to stop until Jessica came home with a
sexually transmitted disease. She had been faithful to him, so
she knew there was only one explanation. The first person she
told was the attorney she hired to handle the divorce. The first
time Robert heard about her disease—and thus his disease—
was when he was served with divorce papers.

The divorce that followed was the first of three. It was after the third that Robert started to realize his life was out of control and it was getting worse. At the worst point of his struggle with sex addiction, he did not care who he had sex with, whether strangers he met or strangers he paid. He sought out sexual connection wherever he could find it.

Life has many strange twists and turns, and God uses them all to draw us to him. So it was when a woman with whom Robert had an affair suggested that he go to the church where I was the teaching pastor. During her own divorce, the woman had returned to faith, gone through a divorce recovery program, and was involved in a Life Recovery group at the church. He was not involved with anyone at the time, and he was full of despair and emptiness. He knew it had to end. He knew he was addicted to sex, but he had not yet found a way out. So, at her invitation, he walked into a Christian church despite his devout atheism. That was when everything started to change.

Until that morning, Robert thought Christians were stupid, naïve, misinformed, or weird. I (Steve) was preaching the morning Robert arrived at church, and the title of my sermon was anything but intellectually stimulating: "The Bible Tells Me So." It was all about the reliability of the Bible and why so many brilliant people believe it to be the written word of God. There was much more to the message, but regardless, the Holy Spirit moved in Robert's heart. By the end of the message, he was convinced that there was a God and that God could help him with his problem.

Before he left church that morning, he had the info on Life Recovery groups. Before the week was over, he joined an Every Man's Battle group. His willingness to go to church as an atheist and to attend a Christian recovery group led to his willingness to turn his life over to the care of God and to accept Christ as his Savior, making Jesus his Higher Power. What an amazing transformation it was from atheist to believer, from active sex addict to working the steps toward sexual integrity.

STEP THREE

*We made a decision to turn our wills and
our lives over to the care of God.*

In Step Three, we truly turn our wills, our ways, and our entire lives over to God, addiction and all. Making this decision seems simple. After all, didn't we commit our lives to Christ? Why wouldn't we want to turn over a shameful addiction after all the painful consequences it has caused? But this is more than salvation and more than asking God to take away our consequences. In Step Three, we intentionally release our hopes, dreams, choices, addiction, compulsions, and relationships, and give God control over all of it. This is a one-time commitment, and it is also the step that opens the door to a lifelong endeavor. We practice it with ever-increasing willingness and trust.

In approaching the decision directed by Step Three, we are challenged to trust God on a deeper level than ever before. Trusting God with everything in our lives may be difficult because of our experiences, from childhood to the present, in which people have repeatedly broken our trust. Life has trained us to be skeptical and wary, to take charge of situations because we don't trust anyone. We may have learned to make life work on our own power because no one around us could be trusted to protect, help, and nurture us. As a result, we can make the mistake of generalizing that lack of trust to God, thinking that he expects us to take care of ourselves, at least in some parts of our lives and issues. Confronting our lack of trust in God's care is critical to working the Twelve Steps in our lives from Step Four through Step Twelve. To have a successful recovery, we must learn to completely surrender ourselves and our wills. As Jesus said, the one who loses his own life for Jesus' sake will find it (Matthew 10:39).

Turning over our addictions and dependencies is definitely like losing our lives. This is our comfort, entertainment, relief, and reward, like a best friend who shares life with us. Letting go of it seems impossible, lonely, scary, and not a lot of fun. "And then to let go of/turn over my will and all my life? I'll have no life left," we cry.

The obstacles of the spiritual realm, our self-will and grandiosity, have held us in the clutches of addiction. They have created the illusion that we are in control. The message and task of Step Three is to face the fact that our control is not real. We may have thought we had control, but God has the ultimate authority and power. When we accept this, then our dependence upon him for the solution to our addiction and any other life problem becomes clear.

Believing that he cares for us can also be difficult. We may have experienced tragedy, abuse, or other suffering that has caused us to lose faith in his care. From our past life experiences, we can draw erroneous conclusions about God and his character. We may try to win his favor by being good, or at least by appearing to be good. Shame about our behavior during our addictive acting-out may have us thinking that we are outside the grace of God, and that he is just waiting to punish us.

So how do we turn our wills and our lives over to the care of a God we do not trust? Our lives are in the balance, wavering between the painful chaos of addictions and dependencies and the offer of new life through recovery. To make this decision, we affirm that we are taking a stand so that we can live. As Moses said in Deuteronomy 30:19, we have a choice to make: life or death. In our case, will it be addiction or recovery? Are we choosing the path that leads to death or to life? Although the life of addiction screams at us to seek perpetual excitement—or perhaps it is numbness we seek—we have to believe that the life God has for us is infinitely better, richer, and more satisfying. We don't have to explain God or understand him; we just need to surrender our lives to him.

As we choose to draw close to God, God brings his reconciling love and redemptive purpose into our lives. In Step

One, we admitted that we do not have power over addiction (or over anything in our lives). In Step Two, we acknowledged that God does have power to heal addiction and to work in our lives. Now in Step Three we decide to turn everything over, let go, and ask for help. These acts of humility allow God's Spirit to draw near to us. When our self-will is out of the way, God can work in our hearts. There may not be immediate results, but in turning it all over to God, we exchange our heavy burdens for the rest and peace that Jesus brings. The weariness of an addictive life can be exchanged for rest. We don't struggle or fight the addiction off. We let go by letting the fight be his; we let Jesus get in the boxing ring with our compulsive desires while we rest on the sidelines, free to do his will. Over time, the obsession is relieved. It's all in God's hands now.

As we choose to give our wills, our thoughts, our decisions, and our behaviors "to the care of God," we rest in the belief that he cares for us. He is with us no matter what life throws at us. With his power and his presence, we are able to stop acting out in the circumstances of our addiction. We are becoming free from the bondage of life-stealing addiction.

The Third Step decision to allow God to take over our whole life is the foundation of subsequent actions we will take to work the remainder of the Twelve Steps.

QUESTIONS FOR **STEP THREE**

Trusting God *Numbers 23:18-24*

1. What in my life has taught me not to trust God?

_____

_____

_____

2. What have I done to cause others not to trust me?

_____

_____

_____

3. What keeps me from surrendering to God?

_____

_____

_____

Free to Choose _Deuteronomy 30:15-20_

1. What is it about my understanding of God that blocks me from deciding to turn my life and my will over to his care?

_____

_____

_____

2. How does fear affect my choices?

_____

_____

_____

Giving Up Control _Psalm 61:1-8_

1. Where did I get the illusion that I can control other people or my circumstances, job, or life?

_____

_____

_____

2. What stops me from giving up my life so that I can find the life God intends for me?

_____

_____

_____

Redeeming the Past _Isaiah 54:4-8_

1. How do I hold God the Redeemer at arm's length? Why?

_____

_____

_____

2. What fears have the most power in my life?

_____

_____

_____

3. How is shame connected to fear in me?

_____

_____

_____

Submission and Rest _Matthew 11:27-30_

1. Why do I think that I am able to handle my addictions/ dependencies on my own with no help from outside myself?

_____

_____

_____

2. How ready am I to be taught?

_____

_____

_____

3. What characteristics interfere with my being taught by Jesus or another person?

_____

_____

_____

Discovering God _Acts 17:22-28_

1. How does my life reflect my image of God at any given moment?

_____

_____

_____

2. How do I define the word _surrender_?

_____

_____

_____

3. What is the difference between "my will" and "my life"?

_____

_____

_____

Single-Minded Devotion *James 4:7-10*

1. What does resistance look like in my life?

   _____

   _____

   _____

2. What do I have to face in myself when I draw close to God?

   _____

   _____

   _____

3. How is addiction connected to my resistance to God's direction in my life?

   _____

   _____

   _____

There comes a point at which we can either merely have faith, or make a bold move and really live our faith. When we live our faith, we no longer just talk about our beliefs but our lives reflect them: What we believe and say and do all line up. But this alignment only happens when we have enough faith to turn everything over to God—every compartment, every hidden secret, everything—and acknowledge, perhaps for the very first time, that God is the Higher Power in our lives.

Prayer for Step Three

Dear God,
I have tried everything but surrendering all that I am to you. Help me to surrender to you today and every day. Help me surrender my problems and my whole self to you. As I come to you humbly, please lift me up as you have promised.
Amen.

PROFILE

I (Steve) live in Carmel, Indiana, a suburb of Indianapolis. Before I lived here, I was a frequent guest speaker for several different organizations. My favorite was called The Gaither Gathering put on by Bill and Gloria Gaither, who are legends of the music industry. They knew everyone in the music world, and once a year they brought speakers and musicians together in Indianapolis for one amazing event. It was through those events that I became friends with Bill. Whenever my phone rang and Bill was on the other end, I knew that we were going to be talking about another musician who was in trouble with sex.

One day Bill called, and within a few hours, I was talking directly with an amazingly talented singer named Jim, who had already achieved significant fame in his early twenties. With his fame came the reality that he not only was a musician, but he was also a highly recognizable Christian representing Jesus to the world. Everyone knew his business, or at least they thought they did. They knew he was married, but they did not know he struggled with sex addiction.

When I talked with Jim the first time, he told me of multiple one-night stands with young women who loved his music. He told me how they came after him, and all they wanted was to get close to a man who sang about God. He made it sound like he was a victim of his admirers. He was not a victim, but he was a sex addict with a lot of access to women who would satisfy his addiction.

When Jim was with these women he had all the power. Instead of using his blessings of fortune and fame to glorify God, he used them to have his way with women who thought he was a man of character and integrity. He left a long trail of hurt and disillusioned young women.

After Jim told me all about his struggles and how he was ready and willing to do whatever it took to get better, I told him, "Jim, nothing fixes everything." It is one of the toughest realities everyone must face if they want to find the life God has planned for them. The history Jim confessed to me had many elements that were not going to be instantly resolved. Even if he were delivered instantly from his addiction to sex by the Holy Spirit, he would not be instantly made into a man of mature Christian character. The hidden wounds that created this love-hungry narcissist would require years of work, not just attending a few meetings for a few weeks. I wanted him to have a realistic view of his future without illicit sex, and if he thought he was not up to the challenges ahead in recovery, he might need to wait.

It's true that nothing fixes everything, and the trouble for Jim and others like him is how difficult it is to know what other things need to be repaired or resolved. That is where Step Four and the searching and fearless moral inventory come in.

Years after our first conversation, Jim shared with me how much that little "nothing fixes everything" phrase meant to him in his recovery. He told me that he discovered that working the steps meant that he would need to do exactly what the fourth step called for him to do in order to find healing. It was the best way to get in touch with all of the hidden wounds that would take more time to heal.

This is what Jim learned through Step Four: Jim's musical talents made him feel special and gifted. He was thankful for this gift, but soon it made him feel entitled. His sense of entitlement made him feel like the rules were for others but not for him. His narcissism was fueled by the increasing attention he received and the deep emptiness it left behind. His sexual behavior went off the rails because there were no rails for him. Like so many, he hoped marriage would fix the problem, and when it did not, he felt entitled to do whatever he wanted.

A large part of Jim's fearless and searching inventory was making a list of the people that he had used. He wrote out what he remembered, including what they had done, how he had felt about each person, and the thoughts that continued to come up. He also included how he had tried to control the damage done to his image and control his sexual partners. It was embarrassing and painful to write out the excuses and manipulations he used to minimize the damage and consequences.

Jim also wrote out what he remembered, thought, or imagined was the impact of his behavior on the people he had used. And for the first time he was able to see that he had used them by selfishly using the power of fame and fortune to draw them in and throw them out. Before Step Four it was all about him, but by working the fourth step his life became all about the others he had hurt and used. Once Jim accepted that "nothing fixes everything" and committed to work on his brokenness for the rest of his life he got his life back.

STEP FOUR

We made a searching and fearless moral inventory of ourselves.

To this point in the Twelve Steps, the work we have done is mostly on our thought processes, attitudes, and beliefs as we have emerged from denial about the seriousness of our problems and our complete inability to change them. We have admitted our powerlessness over our problems, come to believe that God can and will help us escape their effects, and have decided to let go and let God take over our lives. As important as this decision is, it must be followed by action. The remaining nine steps describe the actions we must take to break away from addiction and establish freedom and serenity.

Step Four is the first tangible evidence of internal changes that have been occurring in our hearts as the result of the steps. The first three steps have guided us into growth in humility, and we have trusted God at a deeper level, which is exceedingly important as we face the task of Step Four. It is a fearful and heartbreaking exercise to face the brokenness of our sinful human condition. Most people delay this work indefinitely out of pride or fear, telling themselves that it is a pointless, painful exercise. They might think, *If we avoid practicing the addiction by using the first three steps, then why do we need to look deeper?*

Remember that addiction is threefold: physical, emotional/mental, and spiritual.

It is wonderful and amazing when an addict is able to stop using the addictive substances and behaviors. However, the condition of powerlessness is not just physical. A mental obsession and a pattern of thinking about self and the world traps and tricks the addict into starting up again, even when that person is clean and living a life of sexual integrity! Emotional tirades, intensity of relationships, or even boredom can lead the addicted one to seek relief in the substance or behavior of choice. Thus, spiritually cut off from God, the addict trusts the addictive ritual instead of trusting God to help in handling whatever life has up ahead.

Recovery is the process by which we find new ways of coping and dealing with life instead of using sex and people while avoiding reality. The only way to proceed in that process is to uncover our shame and allow God's light and life to flow in and heal us. We have made a beginning in the first three steps, and now through working Step Four, we find the roadblocks to lasting recovery.

What is an inventory? When a business takes an inventory, it takes stock of what supplies and merchandise are there. Making an inventory shows us what is necessary, what is surplus, what is useless, and what is a liability. Our lives are like a business, and as such, we must take stock of our abilities, qualities, and traits, both good and bad. We must examine our accomplishments and our limitations. In order to stay clean and live with sexual integrity, and develop spiritually and emotionally, we must face even our worst secrets.

At the root of all addiction is our sinful nature, and specifically our selfishness. We want to be on the throne! We want to control the direction of our lives and quite often the lives of those around us. "If they would only do as I tell them . . ." "If they would only listen to my advice . . ." "If they would only use their heads . . ." Our resentments and insecurities grow as we find ourselves unable to have that complete control. If we look at the origin of our problem relationships and difficulties, we almost always find that the root is a decision we have made based on selfish motives. That decision and its resulting action cause us to offend, harm, or betray others—and to invite retaliation. If we are to live in freedom, we must face this fact of our human nature and take continual action to correct such behaviors and any wrongs we have committed.

The basic forms of selfishness in all of us are resentment, fear, pride, envy, dishonesty, greed, and moral or sexual misconduct (lust). All of these will block God's Spirit and make it hard for us to know his will or feel his presence. As these blocks are identified, we can be freed from the burden of trying to look good. The goal is to become more real and honest with people who are in relationship with us.

To be "searching and fearless," we must look at ourselves morally, because God is just and moral. This is difficult when we have been consumed by addiction and mired in self-will. Fear must be put aside, and humility will grow a little as we are willing to document our flaws and misbehaviors. We examine the people, institutions, situations, and events of our lives that have caused us pain and resentment, and we assess our part in them. We do not excuse others of their wrongs, but we see our side of the street. For the first time, we take responsibility for how we have been resentful and fearful, judgmental and critical, negative and isolating. Usually these responses originate from perceived or real threats to our self-esteem, pride, ambition, material or emotional security, and relationships, both acceptable and hidden.

The good news about this work is that we gain an honest picture of ourselves, possibly for the first time. If we weren't so miserable and desperate for a new life, we wouldn't be this gut-level honest. We begin to see patterns of behavior that have caused us trouble time and time again.

If fear is a huge pattern for us, we must turn this over to God. If resentment is our reaction to being hurt or snubbed, we must learn to pray for the person that hurts us. Any resentment, whether justified or unjustified, allows that person to control us, even if he or she has forgotten the incident! Obviously, there is less room for God in our lives if we are controlled by resentments and fears.

Letting go of resentments and fears by working the first three steps on them will banish our irritable, discontented attitudes. Serenity and peace of mind can flow into our lives. Internal changes will become more apparent to others.

After a thorough, searching, and fearless inventory, we can gain a clear understanding of how basing our lives on self has kept us from freely walking close to God. It becomes clear that we have anesthetized the emotional and mental pain of our lives with our addictive substances and behaviors, further cutting us off from him. This first inventory is the beginning of a lifelong practice of self-examination that leads us out of addiction and into relationship with God.

QUESTIONS FOR **STEP FOUR**

Coming Out of Hiding *Genesis 3:6-13*

1. When and in what ways have I led a "double life," looking good on the outside while full of shame about my addiction on the inside?

_____

_____

_____

2. By hiding my problems with image management, how has my shame taken root and grown in my heart? Am I fearful to admit what is there?

_____

_____

_____

3. Am I ready to deal with "the dirt," to wash the inside so I can live free? What holds me back?

_____

_____

_____

4. How has shame driven me into acting out sexually, and how has it sparked the desire to break the cycle?

_____

_____

_____

5. Why isn't a lot of shame enough to transform my life?

_____

_____

_____

Facing the Sadness *Nehemiah 8:7-10*

1. What painful memories keep me from going forward in writing a Step Four inventory? Describe them:

_____

_____

_____

2. What have I been afraid of facing?

_____

_____

_____

3. What role has shame from past mistakes played in keeping me from starting and completing an inventory?

_____

_____

_____

4. Does pride tell me that I don't need an inventory? Have I told myself that others who are in more dire straits than I am are the ones who really need it?

_____

_____

_____

Confession *Nehemiah 9:1-3*

1. What behaviors over my lifetime have been offensive to God?

_____

_____

_____

2. What destructive habits need to be identified and confessed to God?

_____

_____

_____

3. What blocks and resistances do I have to being honest with God about my wrongdoings?

_____

_____

_____

4. What consequences from past wrong choices am I living with today?

_____

_____

_____

5. Am I afraid there may be some unknown future consequences from my sexual encounters in the past?

_____

_____

_____

Family Influence *Nehemiah 9:34-38*

1. Are there people in my family of origin whom I have blamed for my life situations and resulting addiction? If so, who?

_____

_____

_____

2. What resentments do I carry toward them, even if unrelated to addiction?

_____

_____

_____

3. What truly brought me into the bondage of addiction and dependency (what is my responsibility, my part in it)?

_____

_____

_____

4. What specific exposures to sexual things or times of sexual abuse or anything early on may have led me to the path toward sexual addiction?

_____

_____

_____

Finger-Pointing *Matthew 7:1-5*

1. Is it easier to look at the faults and shortcomings of other people in my life, past and present (such as bosses, coworkers, classmates, church members, pastors), than to recognize my own?

_____

_____

_____

2. What is the "log" in my eye, the blind spot that has caused me trouble and given rise to pride, finger-pointing, and eventually to addiction?

_____

_____

_____

3. Where and when have I stepped on people's toes and invited retaliation? Have I been proud, blaming, or fearful?

_____

_____

_____

Constructive Sorrow *2 Corinthians 7:8-11*

1. In what ways have I avoided facing my sorrow about how my addiction has impacted my life and the lives of others?

_____

_____

_____

2. Am I willing to set aside time to grieve and to allow humility to grow in me? When? What is my commitment to myself, my growth, and my recovery?

_____

_____

_____

3. Am I bent on self-condemnation? Am I now willing to let God's mercy go with me as I examine my faults and their impact on others?

_____

_____

_____

God's Mercy *Revelation 20:11-15*

1. Taking a moral inventory of ourselves here on earth will help to prepare us for the life to come. Is anything standing in the way of my taking action, such as pride or fear?

_____

_____

_____

2. As I trust God in Step Three, am I able to let go of pride and fear in Step Four and allow his will to be expressed through me? If so, write out a prayer of trust and willingness to complete Step Four.

_____

_____

_____

3. Write down a list and description of resentments, fears, wrong-doings, and character flaws such as pride, jealousy, domination of others, self-centered needs/wants, etc. (Remember that honesty and humility are character strengths that you are building here, so be as thorough and honest as possible to move toward long-term recovery.)

Fears:

_____

_____

Resentments:

_____

_____

Wrongdoings (actions I have committed that oppose God's standards):

_____

_____

Character flaws:

_____

_____

4. Where have I acted out of pride, vanity, or a sense of superiority?

_____

_____

_____

5. Where and when have I tried to dominate others (e.g., at work, home, marriage)?

_____

_____

_____

6. What makes me jealous, envious, or covetous (wealth, good fortune, successful kids, functional families, jobs, and/or positions of others)?

_____

_____

_____

7. Where and when have I demanded that my wants and/or needs come before those of others, especially those of my spouse, children, or coworkers?

_____

_____

_____

8. After careful self-examination, am I more convinced than ever that I need a Savior every day, not just for salvation, but to walk in freedom from addiction and sin? If so, write out a prayer to God that expresses your complete dependence upon him.

_____

_____

_____

In Psalm 119:29, the writer pleads with God: "Keep me from lying to myself." If we never stop to observe and take note of our patterns from the past, and our defective and deficient ways of coping in the present, we consign ourselves by default to another day of self-deception. The inventory, when compiled with honesty and diligence, is the beginning of facing the truth.

Prayer for Step Four

God,
Help me see who and how I hurt another person. Help me review my reality without shaming myself all over again. Help me be open and honest in the midst of the destruction I have caused and help me be motivated to not repeat the same mistake of forgetting where my true strength lies.
Amen.

PROFILE

Helen was one of the most connected and admired women from her graduating class. She was popular, engaging, and fun—all the things that go with being part of the "in" crowd. It seemed like the sky was the limit for her. She graduated with a degree in broadcast journalism and quickly acquired a job as a reporter for the local television station. Soon she made the leap right onto the anchor desk because she was so bright, engaging, and beloved on the screen.

Helen's experience growing up was not so picture-perfect. Her father seemed like two different men in one body. His public persona loved art and enjoyed a good laugh. He served on the greeting committee at church, and he loved meeting new people. Just like his daughter, he seemed to have it all together and was loved and respected by many people. At home, in private, Helen's father was quite different. He would be happy one minute, and the next he would rage over things that seemed minor. The spells of rage would be followed by long stretches of sadness, no eye contact with anyone, and total isolation.

When Helen came home, she never knew which Dad would be there. Her mom was passive and weak and seemed to always be afraid that the next outbreak of anger was just waiting to happen. She couldn't do anything to encourage him to get help. At the worst of it, Helen's dad physically abused her mom.

In response to the abuse she experienced in her home, Helen

sought out men to date who were intellectual and kind of dull because they were predictable. She fell in love with the ones least like her father. Her first serious relationship did not occur until her freshman year of college. It was through that relationship that her addiction to pornography began.

Helen's college boyfriend seemed safe. He was smart and seemed to know something about almost everything. His consistent demeanor and steady gaze at his solid future allowed her to relax with him. His stable behavior proved to her that he did not have the kind of rage and bitterness inside that would appear when it was least expected.

After dating for a few months, Helen's boyfriend asked her to watch something he found on the Internet. Helen became quickly interested in what she saw. But she did not know why it tapped into something deep inside of her and drew her to it. Her boyfriend showed her a video in which a woman aggressively dominated a man during sex. She enjoyed watching the woman control everything the man did. The connection to Helen's relationship to her father seems clear, but she didn't realize it at the time. She just knew she enjoyed it.

That was Helen's "first date" with pornography. She could not see how dangerous it was at the time or how it tapped into her desire to punish her father for all of the abuse he had put their family through. She was hooked from that first video and could not wait for the two of them to watch more. They watched and then started to act out some of what they watched. No one knew what she was doing except her boyfriend. It was her shameful little secret that grew bigger and bigger. Before long, Helen had a problem she didn't know how to stop. It was mind-boggling to her that beneath her successful, fun-loving façade was a woman who could not stop watching pornography.

At the time there was not much awareness of sexual addiction. Many doubted it was real. Helen says she can't remember learning anything about women with sexual addiction. She struggled on and off with her addiction, sometimes going for months without using pornography, but she always returned to it. It was a huge secret that produced mountains of shame. It cut her off from any meaningful relationship she might have had.

Then her life began to transform. It started with a documentary on women and sexual addiction. There was an interview with a woman who called herself a sex addict. The woman had lost control of her life when she lost her ability to say no to looking at pornography. Just like Helen, it was a boyfriend who introduced her to it. She went on to talk about a group called Love and Sex Addicts Anonymous. There was a phone number for that organization, and a few days later Helen called that number. There was a meeting in her town, but she would be recognized instantly if she went. She found a group that met on Saturdays 150 miles away—outside the viewing area of her network—and she attended her first recovery meeting. She did not say anything while there, but she left with some materials, some phone numbers, and a determination to get a sponsor and work the steps, all the while continuing to live in fear and shame.

She found her sponsor at a meeting a little closer to home. She went to work on the steps, and after Step Four she was ready to share things with her sponsor that she had never shared with anyone else before. She shared them with her sponsor amid many tears and much sobbing. When she was finished, she felt as if she had been hit by a truck. The embrace of her sponsor was so loving and nurturing. Within minutes she felt the burden of her shame lift and leave her. She felt the power of her obsessions and compulsive drive diminish immediately. She was out of hiding and free. She was no longer alone and she was no longer afraid, but Helen was very motivated to continue to work the rest of the steps.

STEP FIVE

We admitted to God, to ourselves, and to another human being the exact nature of our wrongs.

As Christians, we can recognize that Step Five comes from the ancient church discipline of confession. James 5:16 says, "Confess your sins to each other . . . so that you may be healed." We were not meant to keep secrets, even about our most shameful acts. God calls us to be connected, to bear one another's burdens, and to open the eyes of our hearts. Addiction is in opposition to God's design because it thrives on secrets, sneaking, and hiding drinks, hits, or partners. Our first reaction to admitting "to God, to ourselves, and to another human being" is defensiveness and fear. We may decide that since we can see our own faults through the Step Four inventory, and God knows it all anyway, we don't have to be vulnerable to another person.

Such pride and ego block our spiritual growth and keep us at a distance from God and others. Knowledge and understanding alone will never result in recovery. In isolation and protected space, recovery efforts are easily sabotaged, as we create and maintain plenty of room for destructive behaviors to continue. It is easy to keep the veil over our eyes and the eyes of others as we remain in the shadows of denial. Our pride and shame become more ingrained when we avoid facing up to our actions or claiming who we really are.

To work Step Five, we must reach another level of humility and willingness. To have God in all parts of our hearts and lives, we must be able to admit our exact wrongs honestly and openly. By sharing our story of poor choices, poor relationships, and poor reactions to life (i.e., sin), we get a clearer picture of the behaviors we have sown that have led to the harvest of addiction. By being exact and specific, we can no longer fool ourselves about how badly our addiction and its consequences have affected our lives and the lives of people around us. The rationalizing mind of an addict can very convincingly minimize our behaviors. This confessional step initiates a new direction in our lives as we begin living to please the Spirit and harvest everlasting life.

Remember that the steps are not only about victory over

addictive behaviors. They are also about ridding ourselves of the blocks that keep us from being of service to God and others. James clearly says that healing comes from confessing our sins to others, not just from recognizing our shortcomings. In doing so, we cleanse our hearts of resentments, bitterness, fears, and judgments and make room for the truly useful and good things God has for us. Our character assets will be more readily apparent to others and more available to God.

Who should this person be to whom we will entrust our moral inventory? Who can we trust to be part of our healing process? Jesus has modeled for us the type of person we should seek. We need someone who is more interested in our spiritual wholeness and our freedom and progress in recovery than in our individual transgressions. This person must be able to lead us through the shame and the fear while assuring us that getting unstuck is worth the risk of being fully known. Ideally, we can find someone who has been through the Twelve Steps personally, and who can listen with compassion and acceptance, not judgment.

As we read our Step Four "to another human being" in Step Five, our confidante helps us to look even deeper into "the exact nature of our wrongs." In Scripture, we find examples of public confession of sin or wrongdoing that have helped to break down denial of our very human difficulties. By admitting and examining the specifics of our sin as we work Step Five, we find a pathway to the deeper core problems that lead us to wrongdoing. As we come to know the truth about ourselves, "the truth will set [us] free" (John 8:32). A wall that has stood between ourselves, others, and God will come down. We can face our past, mired in addiction, pain, and shame, with a new attitude. A sense of humility and gratitude begins to form. We find that God does not give up on us, and that his compassion is unending. Step Five moves us forward toward freedom.

When we have completed this step, we may have a mixture of feelings, from relief to gratitude to confusion. We have now inventoried and disclosed our deepest moral and spiritual secrets. We have faced some difficult aspects of ourselves that we have wanted to deny before. Adhering to this process is a surrender in itself.

Now we must accept forgiveness from God and our confidante. It is not always easy to simply accept forgiveness—not avoiding or refusing but just receiving. As we do so, we begin to see ourselves in better perspective as being neither better nor worse than others. We are just human beings trying to grow up and get along in the world.

This pathway to freedom, though tedious at times, brings great rewards. Instead of being more self-focused, we become less selfish. Instead of becoming more concerned about our image, we can be more real with others. Instead of being self-destructive, we have a newfound self-respect. Working this step to the best of our ability builds humility and freedom, which continue to grow throughout the entire Twelve Steps.

QUESTIONS FOR STEP FIVE

Overcoming Denial *Genesis 38:1-30*

1. What am I avoiding in Step Four by delaying Step Five?

_____

_____

_____

2. What is the exact nature of my wrongs as listed in Step Four?

_____

_____

_____

3. What interferes with my being honest about myself?

_____

_____

_____

Unending Love *Hosea 11:8-11*

1. How do I react/respond to the truth that God does not give up on me?

_____

_____

_____

2. What keeps me from being truthful with God?

_____

_____

_____

3. What makes me think that I can hide anything from God?

_____

_____

_____

The Plumb Line *Amos 7:7-8*

1. Have my morals and values been in line with God's? Explain:

_____

_____

_____

2. Have I had morals and values without being able to apply them to my life? Explain:

_____

_____

_____

3. What has kept me from staying in line with God's and my own morals and values?

_____

_____

_____

4. Am I ready to surrender to God's moral "plumb line" and share my Step Four inventory? If not, why am I hesitating?

_____

_____

_____

Feelings of Shame *John 8:3-11*

1. What scares me about sharing "the exact nature of [my] wrongs" with another human being?

_____

_____

_____

2. What is my fear related to in my past? How did this fear develop?

_____

_____

_____

3. Has there ever been a time in my life when I felt the fear and took action anyway?

_____

_____

_____

4. Have I set the appointment for completing Step Five by sharing my Step Four inventory?

My commitment to myself:

Date:

Time:

_____

_____

_____

Receiving Forgiveness _Matthew 5:23-24_

1. Why would God want reconciliation before praise when we bring gifts to him?

_____

_____

_____

2. Does anyone have anything against you that needs to be reconciled? Who? Why? What could you do?

_____

_____

_____

3. What would be the impact on your life if you opened yourself up to forgiveness of others and from others?

_____

_____

_____

Freedom through Confession _James 5:16_

1. Lack of confession and openness with others results in a self-constructed prison. Do you know what that is like? Describe it here.

_____

_____

_____

2. How can confession result in such profound healing?

_____

_____

_____

3. Reflect here on God's command to be open not just to him but also with each other.

_____

_____

_____

Escaping Self-Deception _Lamentations 3:40_

1. As I examine myself, can I admit to some self-deception in the past?

_____

_____

_____

2. Does anyone have the freedom to speak truth into my life on a regular basis? Who?

_____

_____

_____

3. Ask three or four trusted friends to write five words describing your strengths and five words describing your weaknesses. Record them here and examine them to discover areas you can work on within your small group of trusted fellow strugglers.

_____

_____

_____

_____

_____

_____

_____

Prayer for Step Five

Lord,
As I share my brokenness with another person, let it be a new
beginning. Give me the willingness to do what I need to do to repair
my heart and my relationships with you and others.
Amen.

PROFILE

Grant was the youngest child, and his parents and siblings would often joke about him being adopted. This joke was not funny to Grant. Every jab or joke increased his feelings of being an unwanted mistake. To hide his true feelings, he would joke back, but he was deeply hurt by their words. Grant felt isolated and detached from his family; his family wasn't really a family.

Since Grant's family was disconnected from his life, he had a lot of spare time to develop some unhealthy habits and attitudes. Watching pornography and masturbating became a daily habit for him. Eventually he regularly brought girls into his bedroom when his family was gone. After he was married, his behavior progressed to numerous sexual encounters with many other women.

At the worst stage of his problem, he continually tried to get better but would fail repeatedly. He was living a lie, and this affected all his relationships. Eventually, he became emotionally disconnected from his children and his wife. He had no self-control.

Grant's wife knew he had struggled with pornography, and she knew of at least one one-night stand years ago. When she finally confronted him about going to a massage parlor secretly, she gave him an edict to either go to an Every Man's Battle workshop and "get fixed," or their marriage was over. Grant called 1-800-NEW-LIFE and signed up for the next Every Man's Battle workshop.

Then he approached a man he knew at his church who had struggled with sexual integrity and asked for his immediate help, because the workshop was still three weeks away. The man told him to get the book *Every Man's Battle* and a copy of *The Life Recovery Bible*. That man became his accountability partner. They started going to a men's Bible study every week, and they attended two Life Recovery meetings before the workshop.

Using *The Life Recovery Bible*, Grant's sponsor and accountability partner took him through the first five steps quickly. The moral inventory took the most time, and when Grant finished, he willingly shared it with his sponsor. The Wednesday evening before he left for the workshop, they met together to discuss Step Six. The timing could not have been more perfect. Grant read it and told his sponsor that he could immediately move to Step Seven because he thought he was ready. His sponsor responded wisely.

Grant's sponsor told him that when he looked over the crummy stuff from Step Four, it would be easy to get rid of the things that are painful to him and others. Step Four does not explore what motivates the pain that he shared. He needed to go beyond his experience of being the youngest child in a disconnected family and examine his actions closer, rather than simply shifting blame. What would it take to stop looking at the past and instead start looking at how he has used that history to excuse his choices? Were there certain patterns of behavior that needed to change?

Grant's sponsor told him to evaluate his level of disclosure and honesty, especially while he was at the workshop. He encouraged him to ask God to help him say the things that he would rather keep from the group. Openness and honesty signals one's readiness for change, while secrecy and distortion would show that he was not ready for God to work in his heart. Finally, he suggested he walk into the weekend with a desire to trust God for the outcome so that he could respond with as much honesty and depth as possible.

Grant did what his sponsor suggested, and his entire week-end at the workshop was all about working through Step Six. He was open and honest and connected well with the other men. Step Six took on a whole new meaning. At first it was easy to say he was ready for God to remove his character defects. He felt like an instant miracle was up ahead. But what he came to understand was that while he could trust God to remove his character defects, he would need to be willing to do more than waiting for a miracle. Those defects would go away by work-ing the Twelve Steps, honestly and consistently, and attending group meetings and counseling. It might not have been the miracle that Grant wanted, but before the weekend was over, Grant was ready for Step Seven.

STEP SIX

We were entirely ready to have God remove these defects of character.

Step Six is a "pause" step. Here we reflect on the infor-mation we have received about ourselves in completing Steps Four and Five—making an inventory of ourselves and admit-ting our faults and shortcomings out loud to another person. We have come a long way in developing a more accurate view of ourselves, in building deeper trust in God, and in recogniz-ing the impact of our addictions and dependencies on our-selves and those around us.

Our work is not done, however. Inventory is just the first half of the process through which, if we are thorough, we will walk away free from debilitating addiction.

Now we must begin to allow God's Spirit to work deeply in our hearts, rooting out our defects of character and making changes in our behavior and attitude that will bring wholeness and serenity.

At first glance, it seems obvious that we would, of course, be ready to have our defects of character removed. Why wouldn't we want to be flawless and blameless? Isn't it our goal in the Christian walk to be perfected in the image of Christ (Romans 8:29)?

Some of our character defects have been useful to us, however, and they have sometimes been necessary for survival. It can be very difficult to let them go when they have been so automatic and so deeply ingrained, but to have a successful, serene recovery, we must let God chisel away even the defects that have been our default mode. This process of becoming "entirely ready" can bring grief—it's like letting go of old friends, and this is painful even when these defects have outlived their usefulness to us and to God. It is important that we take time again to reflect and even grieve about how the disease of addiction has affected us. We may have lost significant time with family and friends because of some of our character defects, not to mention our jobs and reputation.

Facing the brokenness of our sinful human condition is heartbreaking, as David learned in his life. He began as a "man after [God's] own heart" with enough faith to slay giants, but later in his life, he committed adultery and murder. His success in bold acts of faith as a young man led him to believe that he was invincible, or perhaps, after he became king, that laws and rules did not apply to him. Addiction is like that—it can embolden us to act profitably in the beginning, yet it brings grandiosity and arrogance, which lead to our rationalizing the breaking of morals, laws, and rules. As David faced the reality of his sin, he began to see the arrogance of his youth and the value of humility. Such humility before God is forged through "a broken spirit" and a "repentant heart."

One huge character defect for all of us is trying to make life work in our own power. As God says through the prophet Isaiah, "Why spend your money on food that does not give you strength?" (Isaiah 55:2). We often believe, in our self-sufficiency, that if we can only fill this hungry hole in our souls with alcohol, food, sex, money, power, or pornography, we will be satisfied. These turn out to be empty wells, but we keep compulsively running to them. We become addicted and dependent.

In Step Six, we become entirely ready by once more acknowledging that our ways of handling life, even if they have helped us survive in the past, are not what God intends for us. We become ready to have God remove these defects, while acknowledging that we have no power to change ourselves. Here again, we must have our prideful ego dashed if we are to have freedom and serenity. If, after looking at our list of defects, we embark on our own self-improvement program, we may pour a lot of frantic energy into "getting better" and "trying harder" without any real change occurring. The removal of defects is a spiritual surgery that must be accomplished by God's hand. We must let go of the struggle, give over our will on each defect of character, and become open to his work in our heart. Grasping our complete dependence upon him for lasting change takes a great deal of humility and willingness.

However, let us not assume that we are to sit around and wait for God to work magic on us. Becoming ready for him to remove our defects means that we develop humility and willingness and become open to behaving and acting differently. The interaction between Jesus and the crippled man lying by the pool of Bethesda exemplifies this aspect of Step Six. Like this man, we who are addicted have a sincere desire to be healed, to rise up and be productive, and to live a meaningful, purposeful life. We may get ourselves right to the edge of significant progress in recovery, but our character defects have crippled us so that we are paralyzed by fear and cannot get to the next level. We have to let go of familiar patterns that are easy for us even if they are hurtful or debilitating. We may be daunted by the prospect of living in a reality with no anesthetic (our addictive behaviors). It's too risky! Fear of failure, rejection, or abandonment set in, and we sit by the side of the pool, complaining about our helplessness or feeling sorry for ourselves because we must change and work at sobriety.

This step focuses our attention on "being entirely ready," as though Jesus were saying to us: Would you like to get well? As we look inside our hearts, all our excuses, resistance, procrastination, and avoidance of recovery pop up, as they did for this crippled man. Jesus doesn't validate our excuses. He challenged the man to get up, pick up his mat, and walk. Jesus is challenging us in this step "to have God remove all these defects of character." In other words, we are invited to step out in faith, take action toward the recovery behaviors we need to develop, and leave the rest to God. When this man took action, God's healing took place. When we do our part by choosing to act differently in the moment, God removes the defects!

No matter how scary or uncomfortable it may be, we can become willing to take new actions toward fulfilling God's will. We may not feel like being honest where we have been dishonest. We may not feel like being considerate when we have been selfish. We may not feel like courageously facing our problems head-on instead of running from responsibility. But when we become entirely ready, we are willing to allow God to help us to be and to do what we have been unable to do on our own. When we willingly do our part by living rightly in the moment, God removes our defects by supplying his power and his Spirit to make these changes in us. Over time, our defects are replaced with character strengths.

Working Step Six in this way prepares us for Step Seven.

QUESTIONS FOR **STEP SIX**

Taking Time to Grieve *Genesis 23:1-4; 35:19-21*

1. What are the defects identified in Steps Four and Five that are standing in the way of my recovery and service to God? Make a list.

What have each of these defects done for me and against me?

Defect   Positive   Negative

As you look at this list, take some time to grieve. Feel the pain of the losses of both the positive and the negative parts. Some suggestions:

- Write what you will miss about your defects and what you look forward to when these are removed.

- Write what you have learned about yourself in seeing the positive and the negative parts.

- Have a "burial" service. The old has passed away, so burn what you have written, or rip up the list of defects.

_____

_____

_____

Healing the Brokenness *Psalm 51:16-19*

1. How have the last five steps prepared me to be "entirely ready" for God to work in my heart?

_____

_____

_____

2. In this psalm, David had to grow up a little. He had to accept that he was flawed in God's eyes, and that he could never bring a sacrifice good or perfect enough to atone for those flaws. Am I still trying to bring God evidence of how good I am, or am I coming to a place of acceptance, as David did? How does that acceptance help me stay out of my addiction? Explain:

_____

_____

_____

God's Abundant Pardon *Isaiah 55:1-9*

1. In what ways have I tried to fill the hunger of my soul and the thirst of my spirit by acting out sexually instead of trusting and following God's will?

_____

_____

_____

2. Am I ready to turn to God for abundant pardon and for continual nourishment of his Spirit to keep me free of addictive behaviors? Why or why not?

_____

_____

_____

3. Do I believe, not just in my head, that the life God has for me will be more satisfying than the one I have lived under the cloud of addiction? Is my heart willing?

_____

_____

_____

Removing Deeper Hurts *Jonah 4:4-8*

1. What deeper problems did my addiction shelter from my awareness? Pride? Egocentrism? Fear? Anger? Hatred? The arrogance of believing that life should go the way I want?

_____

_____

_____

2. What difficulties have I suffered due to lack of forgiveness or compassion for others?

_____

_____

_____

3. Am I ready to have these defects removed by God? Why or why not?

_____

_____

_____

Discovering Hope _John 5:1-15_

When we are ready, God does what we cannot. Our part is to get rid of excuses, stubborn resistance, holding on to the familiar, and fear of change. When we clear out these blocks and become entirely ready, it becomes clear that God must do the rest, because only he can accomplish the miracle of setting our feet on the path of life again.

1. What have been my excuses for not moving forward in recovery?

_____

_____

_____

2. Have I been stubbornly resistant to becoming entirely ready because I have been afraid of change? Are my defects too comfortable and familiar?

_____

_____

_____

Removed, Not Improved *Romans 6:5-11*

1. What self-improvement tactics and methods have I used to get myself to let go of my addiction and character flaws?

_____

_____

_____

_____

2. Meditate and dwell on the thought that "we are no longer slaves to sin"—nor do we have to remain a captive of sexual sin—"For when we died with Christ we were set free from the power of sin [addictions]" (Romans 6:6-7). Describe the feelings that arise during that time of reflection.

_____

_____

_____

_____

Attitudes and Actions *Philippians 3:12-14*

This is the attitude of Step Six: "I don't mean to say that I have already achieved these things or that I have already reached perfection. But I press on to possess that perfection for which Christ Jesus first possessed me" (Philippians 3:12).

1. Do I have a vision of the purposes for which God saved me spiritually and took me out of addiction? Describe:

_____

_____

_____

_____

2. Am I now willing to accept that I will continue taking this step in order to grow, letting go of the old flaws to make room for the new strengths? Why or why not?

_____

_____

_____

_____

To be ready to battle means that we are appropriately equipped to meet the enemy. When we are ready to allow God to clean things up, there are battles to be fought that require us to be armed and ready. First Peter 4:1 seems to hold the key to what prepares us for battle with our character and its defects. Peter tells us to arm ourselves with the attitude of Christ, who was prepared and willing to suffer. For it is when we are willing to suffer that we are ready to stop sinning. Are you ready?

Prayer for Step Six

God,
I want to be ready for you to do a new work in me. Help me to become willing to do my part so you can do your miracle.
Amen.

PROFILE

Elden tells his story this way:

"I believe that it all started when I fell in love with a good Christian girl who was in my youth group in middle school. We had everything in common and I felt in my heart that she was the one. Yet she never saw me, I felt invisible, and I began to believe there was something wrong with me. My shame grew over time.

"I remember pursuing physical relationships with women I never felt deep connections with, and I remember turning to these 'no strings attached' relationships whenever I felt deep rejection. I started to believe godly love wasn't possible for me.

"After marrying the love of my life, these behaviors didn't go away. They started manifesting again shortly after our wedding. After ten years of this secret life, I had turned to prostitutes, escorts, and physical relationships with coworkers. In my worst moments of shame, after being with one of these women, I would pray for a Gideon Bible to be in my hotel room. I felt God had abandoned me, and I thought about committing suicide. I couldn't face the possibility of my wife and kids knowing who I really was.

"I had deeply betrayed my wife, who already struggled with clinical depression. When I couldn't stop the behavior, I started to realize I was not like other men. The guilt and shame grew to a magnitude that I felt there had to be something wrong with me. I tried everything I could try to change under my own power and self-will, but it never worked. I even started going to Sex Addicts Anonymous prior to telling my wife what had been happening, but that did not work either.

"After attending an Every Man's Battle workshop I started to work the Twelve Steps. Every step brought new insights to me, but it was Step Seven that changed everything. For some people, this is the least significant step because they thought it was a repeat of Step Three or they had been begging God for a miracle all along.

"In the sixth step, I prepared the best I could for God to do something. But the seventh step prepared me in a different way. It was that second word that did it. Maybe I missed something before, but when I saw *humbly* I realized that my getting ready had not focused much on humility. I was ready for God to do a miracle, and I was prepared to ask God to do it with great expectation. I was also ready for God to do it with some entitlement due to the effort I was putting into the meetings and working the steps. And after all, I hadn't lapsed into my old behavior for more than one hundred days. I thought that was worth a reward from God (clearly, I lacked humility). I went to work on the humility before I asked God to remove the shortcomings that just kept coming up.

"I reached the point of healthy humility by writing out all that I thought I deserved after this extended time of being clean. I saw that I really did think that over one hundred days of making unselfish choices—after thousands of days of totally choosing me over everyone else, including my wife and God—I deserved for God to honor my work. When I took the time to go deeper into my thoughts and feelings and expectations, I found this attitude. And that is so bold and conceited to think that God or the world owed me a reward.

"I humbled myself, and once I did, I asked God to remove my shortcomings, starting with my lack of humility. I asked God to help me stop thinking that I am strong enough to change myself on my own or that changing my character will be easy. I asked God to replace my crummy stuff with all of his good stuff, like a love for others and an understanding and acceptance of them. I asked him to give me patience while he made me a better man. There was a shift inside of me, and I started to feel differently about God, myself, my wife, our kids, and our future. I guess it was the beginning of experiencing authentic serenity."

STEP SEVEN

We humbly asked God to remove our shortcomings.

After we have become ready for God to work on removing our character defects, Step Seven is fairly easy: asking him to do his work. When we have truly worked Step Six, we clearly see that our defects have been holding us back from being a channel for God's Spirit. From a sincere desire to be changed inside out, we humbly ask him to remove our shortcomings and build our character.

This is a turning point in our recovery. While we have been focused earlier on stopping the progression of our deadly addictions and compulsions, we must now also let go of the spiritually deadly traits that have kept us from being who we really are. We begin to allow God's Spirit to flow into our lives and replace character defects with character strengths. We get out of our own way, accepting that our way of dealing with life has been problematic for us, others, and God. This is part of the development of humility.

Some of us confuse humility with humiliation. We have been through a lot of humiliating experiences because of our addiction. We have been humiliated by the consequences of addiction, such as jails or broken relationships. We have been humiliated in childhood. Most of us want to avoid being humiliated at all costs, so when the word *humility* is used here, many will not want to have anything to do with it. We have not understood that humility is a quality of spirit that opens the door of our hearts to God. It has nothing to do with humiliation and shame. Humility is an attitude in which we see ourselves in totality, the good and bad parts, the honesty and dishonesty, self-centeredness and self-lessness—in other words, as neither the best nor the worst, just human. Humility is not a sign of weakness; admitting the negative as well as the positive is a sign of authenticity. We become real with God and ourselves.

We may be confused because we have believed in God and had strong religious convictions, yet we have not been able to stop using substances, people, food, or sex. Our Bible studies and prayer meetings have not helped us to curb our angry outbursts at home, our controlling attitudes at work, or our problem with anxiety and fears. This is usually because we have tried to play God, relying on self-will and self-propulsion. Somehow, we think that we must take charge of our recovery, direct our progress, and push for changes. We may even try to whiz through the rest of the steps as if recovery were a race. Our plans, our strategies, and the tactics on which we have depended to get us through life have been nothing more than self-will. We became focused on what we wanted and when we wanted it. Despite our convictions and beliefs, pride and ego edged God out!

Consequently, Step Seven challenges us to embark on the development of our spirits, to let go of directing and managing our image, and to throw ourselves on the potter's wheel to be molded and shaped by his hand, as described in Jeremiah 18. In Isaiah 45:9, an ominous warning comes to Isaiah from God: "What sorrow awaits those who argue with their Creator." If we do not allow God to mold and change us, but still cling to some addictive behaviors such as self-righteous anger or controlling rage, our addiction will eventually return. We must grow and allow God to shape our internal character, or relapse is inevitable.

The awe-inspiring news is that God has a great desire to free us from addictive behaviors and to clean up the resulting character defects: "I restore the crushed spirit of the humble and revive the courage of those with repentant hearts. . . . I have seen what they do, but I will heal them anyway!" (Isaiah 57:15, 18). The only prerequisite is the contrite and humble spirit for which the first six steps have been preparing us.

As we have assessed the damaging effects of addiction on our lives and the lives of others, our desire to be cleansed and molded has intensified. We have found that sexual integrity in itself is a good goal, but to have serenity, solid integrity, and self-respect as well, we must have a change of heart and behavior. With this step, we simply and humbly ask for the removal of our defects and prepare to act differently.

Our first taste of humility was when we admitted our powerlessness over our addiction. Usually, our admission has been the result of repeated problems and humiliations. Now we see that this is just the beginning of a lifelong process in which God brings us closer to his image and purpose.

God will not hammer down the door of our hearts. "Look! I stand at the door and knock," Jesus says in Revelation 3:20. "If you hear my voice and open the door, I will come in, and we will share a meal together as friends." We must open the door by reaching for humility and earnestly seeking to do his will, knowing that depending on our own individual strength is useless. After becoming ready for God to come in (Step Six) and then asking to have our shortcomings removed (Step Seven), we must do our part in the character-building process by putting positive new traits into action. We begin to practice new ways of thinking, behaving, and treating people. Where we have been dishonest, we act honestly. Where we have been selfish, we act with consideration and selflessness. Where we have hidden from responsibility, we face it with courage. Where we have run from conflict, we seek to resolve it peacefully.

When we begin to practice new behaviors, they will feel forced and unnatural, as if we were learning a new dance step with two left feet. If we are intentional and consistent over time, we will be gratified to find that our authentic personality is emerging. As a freshly cleaned cup can hold refreshing water, we are open to God's filling of our spirit. Freedom from addiction will become more automatic, and we will have clearer self-respect as we draw closer to God and to others.

QUESTIONS FOR **STEP SEVEN**

Clearing the Mess *Isaiah 57:12-19*

1. Have I developed enough humility from my experiences in addiction to see that I need to let God work in my heart? Is there any doubt that self-reliance has kept God out?

_____

_____

_____

2. Describe the difference between humiliation and humility:

_____

_____

_____

Giving Up Control *Jeremiah 18:1-6*

1. Have I ever demanded to have circumstances changed for my benefit? When?

_____

_____

_____

2. Have I ever become impatient with God's timing in the process of changing my heart and character?

_____

_____

_____

3. What keeps me from letting go so that God can shape my life better than I could ever imagine or create myself?

_____

_____

_____

Pride Born of Hurt *Luke 11:5-13*

1. Is it hard for me to ask anyone, even God, for help? What keeps me from sharing?

_____

_____

_____

2. What experiences in my family of origin have brought about this self-sufficiency?

_____

_____

_____

3. Have I held back from asking God for what I need because I am projecting my disappointments onto him? Do I trust him?

_____

_____

_____

4. Am I willing to give up self-sufficiency and pride to persistently ask for God's help in removing my shortcomings?

_____

_____

_____

A Humble Heart _Luke 18:10-14_

1. Have I ever compared my faults, problems, and sins to blatant sins of others such as robbery, murder, and adultery to justify avoiding deeper work on my own character defects? What does this do for me?

_____

_____

_____

2. Have I ever justified myself because I attend church, sing in the choir, or do service work? Do I judge others for their lack of participation or involvement?

_____

_____

_____

3. After self-examination in Steps Four through Six, have I been struggling with self-hatred and shame?

_____

_____

_____

4. Do I realize that the "secret sins" of pride, judgment, and comparison are just as serious as the more blatant ones?

_____

_____

_____

5. Have addiction and adversities humbled me enough to open the door to God's forgiveness?

_____

_____

_____

_____

Declared Not Guilty _Romans 3:23-28_

1. Steps Six and Seven are one path to acceptance of this verse: all of us have fallen short, not only of our own ideals, but also of God's glory. Have I been trying to "measure up" and show God that I can "be good" by doing good works? How have I tried to show him that I am okay?

_____

_____

_____

2. Can I now trust in faith that Jesus will not only make up for my weaknesses but will also begin to remove shortcomings as I surrender humbly to his will? If not, why?

_____

_____

_____

Into the Open _Philippians 2:5-9_

1. Have I disguised my addiction by covering it up with a good image? Have I hidden behind a good reputation?

_____

_____

_____

2. Do I still fear that others will find out about my addiction? Will my pride be hurt if someone knows the extent of it? Am I willing to share if it will help others?

_____

_____

_____

3. Can I release to God my self-centered fears of being known and of losing my image? If so, write a prayer to God expressing your desire to do so:

_____

_____

_____

Eyes of Love 1 John 5:11-15

1. God already sees us as we will be when his work is done. Am I aware of any blocks that keep me from asking him into my heart to do that work? What are they?

_____

_____

_____

2. Is my confidence in God's willingness to remove my shortcomings renewed? How and why?

_____

_____

_____

Shortcomings is a very polite way of saying sin, weakness, defects in character, addiction, compulsion, dependency—or a thousand other conditions and symptoms that indicate we are falling short of the glory of God and the lives he has called us to live. Asking God to remove our shortcomings is always a joint venture between us and him. Since we have spent much of our lives proving we can't fix ourselves, it is time to finally ask God to do what we will never have the power or insight to do ourselves.

Prayer for Step Seven

Dear God,
Search my heart and reveal to me any arrogance or pride that is
separating me from you, the people around me, and the person
you have called me to be. My shortcomings are numerous, and my
attempts to fix them always end in failure. Please remove these
shortcomings from me. Do for me what I cannot do for myself.
Give me the courage to do whatever it takes to become victorious
over these problems. Thank you for the work you are doing in me
and for the opportunity to transform my life.
Amen.

PROFILE

These next two steps are the ones that changed my (Steve's) life. No other thing I have ever done has had such an impact on me than working Steps Eight and Nine. Up until the point of working Step Eight I was full of guilt, shame, and remorse. It was hard to look anyone in the eye or to carry on a meaningful conversation because the noise going on inside of me was so loud. I was burdened with fear and shame over a past I could not change. With the discovery of Step Eight, I went from despairing over not being able to change the past to repairing some of the damage I had done in my past.

When I was growing up in Texas, I got a driver's license at age fourteen because I lived on a farm. With that license came a lot of freedom that I did not handle well. Without any constraints or parental supervision, I did what kids with cars did: I went parking with girls whose parents thought I was a nice, responsible young man who had their daughter's best interest in mind. I did some of the time but not always.

Not every relationship I had became sexual. There were so many wonderful young women I dated who I respected and really cared about. I heard about a lot of hurt going on in families, and I had compassion for them. I say all of that to be sure you understand this is about me: My problem was intense at times, but it was in some sort of state of remission at other times. And any judgment should be directed toward me and not someone I dated.

When I heard about Step Eight and what you did with it in Step Nine, I thought it would be the end of working the steps for me. I had already written down and confessed my defects, so refining the list of people impacted by me was not the problem. The problem was thinking of what I needed to do about it after I had completed Step Eight. Reluctantly I started on my list of people I had harmed. The list was a long one.

I started with the people that my early promiscuity had hurt. Since I had been brought up in a Christian home, I knew what was right and what was wrong, but I thought I knew better than what the Bible was teaching when it came to sex. One of the problems was that there were no immediate consequences that I was aware of. It was all about me, so I did not think what the impact on someone else might be, long-term or short-term. It was not long before it became my go-to "drug" to alter my mood. It took me out of isolation, and I felt connected and cared about by another human if I was sexually intimate with her. One day I looked at my life and made the assessment that what I was doing had become everything I knew an addiction could be. For a very long time I knew I could not stop, and I did not want to.

The reality of what I was involved with did not fully hit me until a girlfriend in college told me she was pregnant. Since I was arrogant enough to think that the rules didn't apply to me, I was shocked. I did not give it much thought before doing what I needed to do to stop the pregnancy. I paid for and pressured her to have an abortion so that I could go on with the life I had planned for me. I gave little thought to the woman who wanted to have the baby nor to the life we created. At least I gave little thought until after the abortion, and I realized I had taken the life of my own child. That was when I hit emotional, spiritual, and physical bottom and turned my life over to Christ fully for the first time.

That young woman was at the top of the list of those I hurt. Then there was the unborn baby. After the baby, I continued to list others I had hurt with my sexual behavior. Then I listed those I hurt in other ways by lying to, stealing from, or talking bad about them. When I remembered something I did, but could not remember the name, I would put in blank lines as placeholders for the names. When I was finished with the list, the biggest task of Step Eight was in front of me. The hard part was becoming willing to make amends to them all; I was not willing to do that. It was overwhelming, but I refused to stop moving forward.

Next, I took each name and prayed for them and for insight and wisdom in each situation. Then I wrote down what I could remember about how I hurt each person, trying to not minimize or sink down into shame. Then I wrote down whether or not I knew how to contact them and if I did, how I could do it, whether by letter, phone, or in person.

To reach the point of willingness to make amends to those I hurt, I had to have a good talk with God. I asked God to give me some help in the form of courage. I realized if these steps were stupid, people would have abandoned them a long time ago. If all of them were not necessary, they would have been edited or altered. If I thought I knew more than the thousands that had come before me and worked the steps, then I was right back where I started with my problem, thinking I knew more than God. Since they were not stupid and all were necessary, I was either going to do the hard thing and do this step or I was going to watch my problem get worse. I asked God to add to the courage and for a new outpouring of humility. The courage was there, and the humility showed up too. I was finally ready to make amends to them all.

STEP EIGHT

We made a list of all persons we had harmed and became willing to make amends to them all.

In our journey through the Twelve Steps, a spiritual awakening forms the purpose of healing our relationships with self, others, and God. To be free from addiction, we must be willing to go to any lengths to achieve this spiritual healing. Step Eight is crucial to living out this goal, even if we feel threatened by the possibility of facing our most difficult relationships.

We have been in the midst of transforming our thinking, behaviors, and attitudes. Our pride and false self have been punctured to reveal the new "skin" of a humble, teachable spirit.

However, considering Step Eight may activate our egos and defensiveness once more. Just imagining having to make amends to some of the painful relationships of the past can activate fear of the possible humiliation in store when we contact these people. "It's in the past; it's over and done with; nothing can be changed now," we will want to protest. Of course, we also want to point out to our sponsors and trusted advisers that these are people who harmed us. "When do they have to make amends?" we cry. All these excuses are ways to resist forgiveness. We may fear that other people will perceive that we condone their behavior, or that we are allowing others to take advantage of us.

But if we are to achieve lasting recovery from addictive substances and behaviors, forgiveness is required. Step Eight requires the shattering of our pride once again, to develop deeper humility that opens the way to forgiveness. God expects us to extend mercy to other people, just as God has extended mercy to us. (See the parable of the unforgiving debtor in Matthew 18:23-35.) Unless we transcend our own hurts and have mercy on others who have harmed us, we will remain in the prison of our addictions. Lasting recovery and serenity will continue to elude us.

To make our list, we first have to identify and admit the harm we have caused others. There are many other excuses, but we are now going to be even more drastic in taking responsibility for ourselves because we want spiritual freedom. Although it is challenging, we must now examine our unintentional sins and how unaware we have been of the harm we have done to others. We have not allowed ourselves to be aware of the fact that our sex addiction (and other addictive substances and behaviors) affects our moods, emotions, and judgment. The harm may not be tangible, but it is damaging nonetheless. What about family members who suffered our silent scorn, pouting, or depressive bouts? What about the emotional effects of our angry tirades? What about subjecting our family to our poor judgment with money, time, decisions for work, or moving from city to city? Thinking along these lines, we can see that our list may be quite extensive.

This step is only for list-making and for becoming willing to make amends. We must work with our sponsor to reach a decision about whom we will make direct amends to when we work the next step. If we put off making our list because we are thinking of Step Nine, then we are not fully engaged in the task of Step Eight.

Whether we have made poor choices under the influence or have just been insensitively unaware of our effect on others, in Step Eight we become willing to amend our ways and take responsibility for ourselves. We may put off working this step because we are afraid of the responses we will get. We are not responsible for how they respond, only for our willingness to set the relationship right.

Our resentment and defensiveness—natural responses to unhealthy relationships—will block us from offering forgiveness to the people on the list. We may have to review Step Four for our part in these situations. Through the prophet Hosea, God described the law of sowing and reaping: "Plant the good seeds of righteousness, and you will harvest a crop of love. Plow up the hard ground of your hearts, for now is the time to seek the LORD, that he may come and shower righteousness upon you" (Hosea 10:12). Steps Four through Nine are actually for "plowing up the hard ground of [our] hearts."

As we become clear about our responsibility for our crop of anger, grief, and sadness over broken and lost relationships, we can be more open to the process of making amends. The "plowing up" that occurs by taking these steps and seeking God's will is actually the beginning of a new crop of forgiveness and compassion toward those we have hurt and those who have hurt us. We may still have to face negative consequences from our addictive behaviors, but our heart work will become life-changing recovery. Realizing that our own wrongdoings have been forgiven and that we are on a path of new life, we are more apt to offer forgiveness and understanding to others. This act of humility and forgiveness opens us to the willingness to make amends.

One more thing: Often when we make a list of people we have hurt, we leave off the person who has experienced more pain than anyone else—ourselves. It might be helpful for you to acknowledge that you have hurt yourself and to put your name at the top of the list of people you have harmed. Willingness to forgive ourselves and make amends to ourselves makes it easier to do the same for others. One day of sexual integrity is a powerful way to make amends to yourself.

Take your time with your list, and then we will be ready for Step Nine.

QUESTIONS FOR **STEP EIGHT**

Making Restitution *Exodus 22:10-15*

1. How have I failed to respect the personal boundaries or the personal property of others?

_____

_____

_____

2. Is there a particular person who has been hurt repeatedly by my irresponsibility?

_____

_____

_____

3. What excuses have I used for not looking at my behaviors?

_____

_____

_____

Unintentional Sins _Leviticus 4:1-28_

1. In what areas have I unintentionally harmed others with my words, moods, self-pity, depression, anger, or fears?

_____

_____

_____

2. In what ways have I acted thoughtlessly without regard for others' needs or feelings? When? To whom?

_____

_____

_____

Scapegoats _Leviticus 16:20-22_

1. Have I been putting off making a list because I am afraid of some responses? Whose?

_____

_____

_____

2. Have I held on to shame about a certain incident or relationship? What am I willing to do to let go so that I can become willing to make amends?

_____

_____

_____

3. Is there someone I am having trouble forgiving who blocks my willingness? Who?

_____

_____

_____

Overcoming Loneliness *Ecclesiastes 4:9-12*

1. How have I allowed isolation due to shame and guilt to keep me from supportive relationships?

_____

_____

_____

2. What is the role of shame and guilt in my isolation and acting out?

_____

_____

_____

3. Am I willing to forgive myself for the hurt I have caused others? Write a prayer of willingness to forgive and ask for God's grace to heal these relationships.

_____

_____

_____

Forgiven to Forgive *Matthew 18:23-35*

1. Are there people on my list that I am having trouble forgiving for their part in our relationship? Who and why?

_____

_____

_____

2. What keeps me from letting others off the hook? Fear? Resentment? Caretaking?

_____

_____

_____

3. What blocks me from forgiving others for the wrongs done to me?

  a. Fear of what others would think of me? (Pride?)

_____

_____

  b. Fear of letting others see my hurts?

_____

_____

  c. Fear of conflict? Protecting others' feelings to avoid conflict?

_____

_____

The Fruit of Forgiveness _2 Corinthians 2:5-8_

1. Is there anyone on my list I am refusing to forgive and it is blocking my willingness to move forward in making restitution?

_____

_____

_____

_____

2. Am I willing to let go of judgment and disapproval to open myself to working this step?

_____

_____

_____

3. Have I been so afraid of rejection that I have delayed willingness to make amends? Who could reject me and why?

_____

_____

_____

Reaping Goodness _Galatians 6:7-10_

1. What "crop" did I sow while practicing my addiction?

_____

_____

_____

2. Describe the correlation between healthy living and acceptance.

_____

_____

_____

Prayer for Step Eight

Lord,
Help me to see the people I have harmed and give me insight into
how to make what I've done wrong right.
Amen.

PROFILE

After I (Steve) made my list, I set out to make direct amends. I met in person with some, and I called others on the phone. I did not know what their response would be, so I did not invite them to eat with me or even have a cup of coffee. Here was what I said when I made contact: "I know we have not spoken in a while, but there is something very important I would like to share with you. Could I come by and talk to you for a few minutes?"

If there was a hesitation, I went right into, "If you would rather I share it with you now, I could do that." If I called and left a message, I said both of those parts in the message. Most people just wanted to talk on the phone. When I apologized, I said something like this:

> I have been making some changes in my life and a big part of those changes has been looking back on some relationships and realizing that the impact of who I was and what I did was hurtful. I thought of you, and I am so sorry for what I did in the past. I want to ask you to please forgive me for the way I treated you, and I understand if you are not willing to do that.

Then I uncomfortably waited for their reply.

The replies usually went like this: "I can't believe you are doing this. Of course I forgive you." "Yes, I forgive you, and I hope you will forgive me also." "Oh, no one has ever done this before, and I can't thank you enough for calling. Yes." There was not one person that I spoke with that was anything but forgiving. Their forgiveness was immensely healing.

Then I would thank them and ask if there was anything I could do for them to make it right or make up for what I had done. Then I would ask, "How are things going with you?" or "Is there anything you would be willing to tell me about your life now?" But I did not want to be an intrusion or act like I was in any way entitled to any more of their time or information. I also did not ask to pray with them, or tell them I would be praying for them, or ask them to pray for me. Why? Because I did not want them to think that I was trying to look or act or be extra spiritual. I just wanted to ask for their forgiveness, and that was enough.

To others I wrote letters, and they were similar to my phone calls. They were not long, but if I remembered something specific about what I had done, I would include it. I simply told them I was making some changes, wanted to make things right, remembered them, and asked for their forgiveness. I might give an e-mail address or phone number if they wanted to contact me. I might also enclose a self-addressed, stamped envelope and blank card. When I did that, I usually got a short note back saying thank you and that they forgave me. It was all so powerful and freeing. This experience transformed me.

When I began this process, I knew that God had forgiven me. I had accepted his forgiveness. I believed Christ's sacrifice paid the price for all of the things I had done. I would say I had forgiven myself, but I still carried residual shame and guilt. I think that was there because knowing I was forgiven was not enough. I really did need to do what I could to make things right, and it was this ninth step that allowed me to live into the freedom I already had. That is why I am so grateful for this step.

I was also grateful for the warning not to cause further harm.

But I was also cautioned not to use that as an excuse to do nothing. Too often someone starts making amends in the absence of a direct amends because they are afraid or unwilling. Sometimes they fear they will lose their control over the other person's response. But the other person deserves to know the truth. Making amends probably will result in a loss of control because no one should be in control (that's what these steps are all about). Consider carefully your next moves so that you don't hurt anyone. But don't continue to hurt yourself or someone else by using it as an excuse not to do what is right.

STEP NINE

We made direct amends to such people wherever possible, except when to do so would injure them or others.

In Step Nine, we put into practice the principles of the first eight steps: powerlessness, restoration to sanity, surrender, inventory of wrongs, willingness, and seeking help. To all this we add making amends.

The word *amend* means "to change." This is not an apology step of groveling self-humiliation. Instead, it is admitting to the people we have wronged that we know and understand the pain we have caused, and that we are committed to changing our behavior so that we will avoid causing any more pain. This step is about direct amends wherever possible, so we will go to these people personally or write them a letter. When we are face-to-face with these people, we need to have the previous steps' principles at work in us to be able to accomplish our goal.

Why would we put ourselves at such risk of exposure and shame? Step Nine offers us the opportunity to become free from the past. We can heal our relationships with others, with God, and with ourselves. In Genesis 33:1-11, we see this step in action as Jacob offered financial amends to his brother,

Esau, by sending flocks of livestock before they met face-to-face. He was totally fearful of Esau's reaction to seeing him again after all the deception and thievery Jacob had practiced at Esau's expense. Jacob had to experience being deceived himself before he gained enough humility to recognize his faults.

The positive, healing outcome of this relationship was years in the making. In the same way, we have been through the pain of addiction, and now we are on a path of recovery that takes time. We must be willing to accept whatever response we are given. We must be willing to repair and resolve whatever has broken down in the relationship, even if the other rejects our offer to do so. As with Jacob, our willingness to go the extra mile is part of the spirit of Step Nine. The gifts Jacob sent to Esau were part of making restitution for the injury he had done and an expression of humility for his wrongs.

In Step Nine, we also become more realistic about ourselves and clean our side of the street, so to speak. When we are willing and open, God seems to give us a nudge to remind us of past promises on which we have not followed through. We may have damaged others' trust in us. We may have had extensive intentions, yet we can show no tangible evidence of those big plans and ideas. David had the experience of remembering an unfulfilled promise, as recorded in 2 Samuel 9:1-9. Like David, we need reminders of promises we have left unfulfilled. Step Nine gives us the assignment of remembering and acting on this.

Making direct amends wherever possible really challenges us to take opposite action from what our addictive personality would do automatically. Addictive behavior would be to cover up, hide, and avoid seeing anyone who might be angry with us or upset by our actions. Jesus challenges us in the Sermon on the Mount:

> So if you are presenting a sacrifice at the altar in the
> Temple and you suddenly remember that someone has

something against you, leave your sacrifice there at the altar. Go and be reconciled to that person. Then come and offer your sacrifice to God. When you are on the way to court with your adversary, settle your differences quickly. Otherwise, your accuser may hand you over to the judge, who will hand you over to an officer, and you will be thrown into prison. (Matthew 5:23-25)

Jesus knows that if there is a broken relationship with resentment on one or both sides, we are not spiritually free to worship God. The harmed person could also put that resentment into action and create great pain for us in retaliation. In other words, spiritual and physical bondage are the consequences of harming others with no attempt to repair it. When we learn to set right, to the best of our ability, the situations in which we have caused hurt, and actually change our behavior to stop the harmful results, we are turning from the old addictive pattern to new recovery behavior.

Step Nine places an astounding call on our lives to repair our relationships, transform our inner self, and learn a new way of living. In Ezekiel 33:10-16, there is a list of amending actions: to return what was stolen, to obey God's life-giving laws, and to stop doing what is evil. When we confront the utter self-centeredness that has motivated the actions, drives, goals, and feelings of our lives, we may be daunted by the enormity of the recovery life. We may wonder whether this new life is really possible for us. We may have observed people who have attempted recovery from addiction, only to return to drinking, overeating, and acting out sexually. We may wonder if continual recovery is possible.

Our response must be to allow God to do his work in us by surrendering the outcomes and simply taking action. Recovery is possible if we stay the course and take one day at a time.

Working the first eight steps creates a readiness and willingness to assess our past mistakes, even when this is uncomfortable. In Step Nine, we actually take action to correct them. In

Luke 19:1-9, Zacchaeus came to Jesus and was inspired to take an inventory of himself. He recognized that he had harmed others as a part of being a tax collector for the Roman government. When he realized this, he publicly promised Jesus that he would amend his wrongs and make restitution for them. Jesus commended his attitude and actions as evidence of his spiritual change (i.e., salvation). This demonstrates the critical importance of Step Nine. We are in the process of spiritual development, and making amends is the first public display of our recovery from addiction and sin.

The amends process will often present situations that call for financial restitution. How will we respond? Zacchaeus made amends by giving away half of his wealth. Then he gave more to people he had cheated, face-to-face. This is an example of direct amends.

The person who can make direct amends visibly shows humility, compassion, and the realization of his place before God. Salvation comes as we start to think more of others than of ourselves.

The amends process in Steps Eight and Nine brings out the "unfinished business" in our lives. We may discover past traumas that must be faced and dealt with if we are to maintain our recovery. We need to talk to our sponsor, counselor, or other trusted adviser so that we are not working with such issues alone, but they must be dealt with and resolved or they will follow us daily as though we were chained to them. We may not have caused or asked for these traumas to occur, but we may have to make amends to ourselves for playing the victim or curtailing our lives as a result of trauma. Step Nine allows us a new kind of freedom with ourselves, other people, and God.

Restoration of relationship with self is an important outcome of Step Nine. There is no more need to run when we have come face-to-face with those we have harmed and sought to make things right with them. We no longer need to run because the slate is clean. We no longer need to speculate about forgiveness—we have forgiveness.

As we allow Step Nine to work in our lives, a new set of attitudes begins to emerge. Because of the life-changing relationship with God they developed, the first one hundred alcoholics to follow the Twelve Steps found that they could promise these results:

> We are going to know a new freedom and a new happiness. We will not regret the past nor wish to shut the door on it. We will comprehend the word serenity and will know peace. No matter how far down the scale we have gone, we will see how our experience can benefit others. That feeling of uselessness and self-pity will disappear. We will lose interest in selfish things and gain interest in our fellows. Self-seeking will slip away. Our whole attitude and outlook upon life will change. Fear of people and economic insecurity will leave us. We will intuitively know how to handle situations which used to baffle us. We will suddenly realize that God is doing for us what we could not do for ourselves. (Reprinted from *The Big Book*, pages 83-84, with permission of A.A. World Services, Inc.)

When we work the Twelve Steps to the best of our ability, they become realities in our hearts and lives. These are the changes we can expect when we earnestly seek the spiritual structure for life described in the Twelve Steps.

QUESTIONS FOR **STEP NINE**

Long-Awaited Healing *Genesis 33:1-11*

1. Who are the people on my Step Eight list who strike the most intense fear in my heart when I think about making amends face-to-face?

_____

_____

2. Do I have supportive people to help me gain willingness to take such a challenging step? Do I have an adviser or sponsor to work with me?

_____

_____

_____

Keeping Promises 2 Samuel 9:1-9

1. How have my thoughts, opinions, and ideas affected the decisions I have made?

_____

_____

_____

2. Is there anyone to whom I owe amends due to forgetting, either on purpose or unintentionally, to fulfill a promise?

_____

_____

_____

Covering the Past Ezekiel 33:10-16

1. What forms of harm listed in Step Eight do I resist giving up in order to make amends with another?

_____

_____

_____

2. What fears keep me from the life-giving process of Step Nine?

_____

_____

_____

Making Peace *Matthew 5:23-26*

1. What is my usual response or reaction to brokenness?

_____

_____

_____

2. Does my amends list include people that have something against me? If so, do I have difficulty finding the courage to deal with them?

_____

_____

_____

From Taker to Giver *Luke 19:1-10*

1. List financial amends that you owe. Name the people and amounts:

_____

_____

_____

2. Am I willing to go to any lengths to offer amends? What risks are involved?

_____

_____

_____

Unfinished Business *Philemon 1:13-16*

1. How far will I go to restore a relationship with another person, with God, and with myself?

_____

_____

_____

2. Do I have any unfinished business left on my list? List these categories:

Money owed to people, jobs, businesses:

_____

_____

Any laws broken:

_____

_____

Broken, painful relationships:

_____

_____

3. Am I waiting for the certainty of forgiveness before I make amends? Am I willing to take the risk? Explain.

_____

_____

_____

A Servant's Heart *1 Peter 2:18-25*

1. What am I afraid will happen when I attempt to make amends?

_____

_____

_____

2. Do I fear that painful consequences will cause me suffering if I make amends? If so, what is the worst that could happen?

_____

_____

_____

3. Do I trust God's will for me if I follow the challenge of Step Nine?

_____

_____

_____

4. Which of the Twelve Steps do I need to focus on before I make these fearsome amends?

_____

_____

_____

It's one thing to say you are sorry. It's another thing to prove it. Anyone can make a phone call and ask for forgiveness. At least they can enter the recovery process that results in confessing wrongs to another person and asking forgiveness. But it is the courageous person of character who wants to right the wrong, restore the loss, or pay back what was taken or owed in any way possible. Making amends is a powerful way of setting things straight, and it leaves others better equipped to do what you have asked: forgive you. There is a price to be paid for freedom.

Prayer for Step Nine

Lord,
Give me the courage I need to ask for forgiveness. Give me the
character to make things right with the people I hurt. Help me to be
responsible in all areas of my life and in no areas of another person's
life. Help me to make appropriate amends and walk free.
Amen.

PROFILE

Theresa was raised in a very loving home but without healthy boundaries or limits, so she was sexualized at a very early age. Her mother was naked most of the time, and she openly watched pornography, adult movies, and masturbated. She encouraged Theresa to behave the same way, and she had no other family around to tell her otherwise.

By age twelve, Theresa was watching porn and masturbating frequently. She just thought this is what you do when you are free and not uptight. When she started having boys over to the house, her mother would not worry about what they did. There were no rules about sex other than to be sure to use protection during intercourse. Her behavior resulted in a lot of boys hanging out at her house, and her being involved sexually with many of them.

As she grew older, she continued to have many sexual relationships with many men. She could not have enough men or enough sex in her life. Nothing fulfilled her the way sex did. She drank more and more and dabbled in drugs, and everything continued to be worse than it had ever been before. Like so many addicts, she wondered if her addiction would end with her death.

For Theresa, it ended with her in the emergency room because a random sexual encounter with a man turned violent. He beat her badly, and she had no idea who he was or where he went. The female police officer assigned to her case helped her take the step toward recovery. She told Theresa that, at one time in her own life, she had been where Theresa was now, and she had sought help at a recovery meeting of Sex and Love Addicts Anonymous. The officer offered to take her to a meeting, so when Theresa was better, she went with the officer. That was the beginning of her transformation.

Theresa began working the steps, and shortly after her celebration of one year of being pure and clean, she met a nice man. On their first date, she told him about her standard of abstaining from sex before marriage. Theresa worried that he would be bothered, but instead he loved it. Theresa had mixed emotions. She was glad he didn't want to date her just for sex, but she feared how a good man like him would react when he found out everything about her past.

They continued to date, and she continued to work her program. Eventually, he told her he wanted to spend the rest of his life with her. So, she had to disclose all that she had done. She made sure he understood the Twelve Steps and how they had changed her life. She wanted him to focus on Step Ten above all. He told her that it was evident that she had been practicing this step with him. She told him that he could count on her adhering to and practicing this step and the others for the rest of her life. Then she told him everything. It was a painful disclosure but she left nothing out.

When she was done, he was weeping. He knew she had a tough past, but he did not know how desperate she had been. But instead of judgment, he had compassion. Rather than fear, he had confidence that they could share a good marriage. One year later they married. They included Step Ten in their vows. That was the beginning of a very happy marriage.

STEP TEN

We continued to take personal inventory, and when we were wrong, promptly admitted it.

Step Ten is the first of the "maintenance steps." We have faced our powerlessness and utter dependence upon God for our recovery and serenity. We have assessed our assets and liabilities for our usefulness to God and others. After clearing away the debris left by the effects of the choices we made and the acts our addiction pulled us into, we are ready to accept that the underlying principle of working these Twelve Steps is spiritual character building rather than comfort and convenience. We are coming to accept that our purpose here on earth is to do the will of God more and more completely, but we will not be able to grow spiritually in recovery without working this step continuously.

The concept of this step is similar to the rigorous exercise program that marathon runners use to prepare for their events. A marathon is a strenuous mental and physical challenge, and success requires focused, purposeful energy. Recovery is also a marathon, a strenuous challenge that requires similar purposeful, focused energy to achieve. No one can prepare for a marathon in a day, and we are reminded we must take one day at a time with consistent discipline to assure continuous sobriety and serenity. Step Ten allows for planned, disciplined time to develop spiritual strength and agility.

For many of us, physical exercise is hard to do consistently. We may complain that it seems boring and tedious. To continuously take personal inventory may also seem tedious and needless, a real downer when we want to enjoy our recovery. These are defects of ego and pride that are part of our sinful nature. The disease of addiction can use them to keep us from long-term recovery.

By adopting this spiritual exercise, we practice regular ego/pride deflation that allows humility to continue to develop in our souls. The rewards are often delayed, but we are laying the foundation for staying sober and clean under any circumstances. We need to search ourselves spiritually to identify addictive thinking and out-of-control emotions before they throw us off balance. If we assess our defects as they arise, we can correct them promptly and stay on the path of recovery.

Step Ten is also written to remind us that we are human beings and that we will frequently be wrong! The step does not say "if" but "when" we are wrong. This also levels our pride and helps to keep us emotionally right.

The word *promptly* is written in this step for the addictive self in us that recognizes wrongs and faults, but delays in letting anyone know because of pride or ego. If we promptly admit and correct ourselves, we prevent the diseased thinking from taking hold in our minds and hearts, and we stay close to God. In the book of James, healing is said to occur when we confess our sins to one another (see James 5:16).

We must never weary of taking Step Ten. Each day we can do spot-check personal inventories and push toward spiritual growth. This diligence allows us to achieve continuous sobriety and serenity. When we suffer, we often grumble and complain, asking "why me?" We may resist having to take inventory of ourselves again, but admission of faults and willingness to correct our wrongs bring eternal rewards in the spiritual realm. In other words, the labor involved is worth the suffering and the ego-puncturing that result from working the Twelve Steps, especially Step Ten.

After achieving sobriety and being clean for a time, we may think that all of our other defects should be taken care of once and for all. This would mean that we have no sin and we are fooling ourselves! "Continuing to take inventory" and admitting our faults allow humility to grow in our character as God does the forgiving and cleansing and shows that his Word has a place in our hearts. Where our addiction once made us oblivious to our wrongs/sins, our conscience is being restored. God's Word lives in us, and we recognize our need for him.

We may notice that the concepts and the work of the last six steps are actually rolled into this one step: inventory; confession; recognizing defects, faults, and sins; and making amends. This is our new blueprint for living—our path through the woods of life. The continual loop of self-examination and the development of humility propel us into greater serenity and deeper connection with God, self, and others.

QUESTIONS FOR **STEP TEN**

Personal Boundaries *Genesis 31:45-55*

1. In order to restore trust in relationships, what particular vulnerabilities do I need to set boundaries around?

_____

_____

_____

2. Is there a trusted person to whom I can clearly define my commitments? Who? What commitments am I willing to make?

_____

_____

_____

Repeated Forgiveness *Romans 5:3-5*

1. Do certain behaviors and character defects that show up in my Step Ten inventory point to a pattern? Which ones? What is being revealed about me?

_____

_____

_____

2. Am I having trouble admitting these promptly and forgiving myself?

_____

_____

_____

3. Do I give myself grace? Why or why not?

_____

_____

_____

Dealing with Anger _Ephesians 4:26-27_

1. What is my first response when I am angry? Lashing out? Stuffing down? Avoidance and covering up?

_____

_____

_____

2. How was anger dealt with in my family? How did my mother deal with anger? My father? Which pattern do I follow?

_____

_____

_____

3. When I am angry, can I promptly admit it? Why or why not?

_____

_____

_____

4. Do I have support people who can help me learn to deal with anger more appropriately? Am I willing to ask for assistance with this issue?

_____

_____

_____

5. Do I see how anger drives my entitlement, lust, and coveting something that I do not possess or someone that is connected to someone else?

_____

_____

_____

Spiritual Exercises *1 Timothy 4:7-8*

1. As this continual inventory is important for spiritual fitness, where in my daily routine can I set aside time to make self-assessment part of every day?

_____

_____

_____

2. Do I have any resistance to evaluating my defects daily? What are my objections? What do I fear?

_____

_____

_____

3. An example of a simple, daily, personal inventory:

Where have I been selfish, dishonest, fearful, inconsiderate, or proud?

_____

_____

What have I done right today?

_____

_____

What do I need God's help with tomorrow?

_____

_____

What am I grateful for today?

_____

_____

Perseverance _2 Timothy 2:1-8_

1. How do I see my recovery as a war against addiction and as a fight for my soul?

_____

_____

_____

2. How do I see myself as an athlete training for the marathon journey of recovery and serenity?

_____

_____

_____

3. Am I working in every season and situation, planting seeds of recovery by applying the Twelve Steps to my life?

_____

_____

_____

4. Where do I lose heart in fighting, training, and working through the Twelve Steps?

_____

_____

_____

Looking in the Mirror *James 1:21-25*

1. Have I been quick to recognize but not take action in a particular area of my life or defect of character? If so, I can take action without self-criticism by going back through Steps Six and Seven, then Eight and Nine on that particular area or defect. What is the area that needs attention, and how often does it become an issue?

_____

_____

2. On what area or defect do I need to take action today? This week? This month?

_____

_____

Recurrent Sins *1 John 1:8-10*

1. Have I hoped for immediate release from my defects, as I may have had from my addiction? Have I perhaps unknowingly hoped that by doing all this step work I could attain perfection? Write any thoughts and feelings that arise from reading this meditation:

_____

_____

_____

2. Am I clear that I still need inventories to continue my spiritual growth? In other words, have I developed enough humility to accept that inventories will be a regular part of my journey? Explain:

_____

_____

_____

3. Am I sensing that my conscience is returning or developing so that I more easily recognize my faults? Am I humble enough to admit them more readily? Record any progress you've noticed in your conscience:

_____

_____

_____

Our lives require an ongoing evaluation of our thoughts, deeds, desires, and motives. As long as we live in the time between the Garden of Eden and heaven, we will always have times when we need to stop what we're doing and search our souls for areas that need additional attention. We also need to evaluate our relationships and interactions with others and admit to ourselves that we've been wrong. When we admit that we've been wrong to the person whom we have wronged, we initiate reconciliation and open the possibility of a deeper connection. Admission of a wrong is not evidence of a lack of recovery or a weak recovery. In fact, a humble heart and honest confession have always been the hallmarks of successful recovery. Our recovery is never stronger than when we are open, honest, and humble enough to admit we have made a mistake.

Prayer for Step Ten

Dear Lord,
Help me to stay humble enough to see others and willing enough to see how my behavior impacts them. Help me to be courageous enough to admit when I have made a mistake and hurt another person. O God, may I never be deceived to think I do not have serious work to do. Amen.

STEP **11**

PROFILE

Jack was in his third marriage when his wife at the time found out something about him his other two wives had already discovered. Jack had a double life where he watched gay porn and occasionally relapsed into sexual encounters with men. His wife found the pornography on his phone, and that was when Jack confessed everything to her. He told her that he would do anything to save their marriage and that he had been dealing with his issue already. He sought counseling over this issue, and he attended Life Recovery meetings. He was mostly successful in staying pure and clean, but he relapsed over and over again. He promised that if she would stick with him, he would figure out what was missing from his recovery program.

She agreed, and they began working on Jack's treatment together. They started seeing a marriage counselor who was familiar with sexual addiction. He saw the same counselor on his own, and he increased his support group meeting attendance. Jack really did want to get better and to honor his wedding vows.

Jack had heard of men in his support group who found that they could be free from the obsession and compulsion and not relapse. Determined to figure out why he relapsed, Jack set aside a time to talk to each one after the meeting and alter his plan to look more like theirs. Everyone he talked to focused on one phrase that had been the key to their recovery and maintaining a pure and clean life of sexual integrity. The phrase was "God, as we understood him."

Each person understood God in a very different way when they started recovery: angry, distant, uncaring, punitive, and dangerous. But throughout their recovery experiences, they had found that God might be and probably was totally different than they originally understood him. They decided to pursue a God who had a different, more loving character. When they started to work Step Eleven, they made a solid commitment to improve their relationship with God and their contact with him. They prayed to know his will. They prayed for power to do his will. God became real to them through Step Eleven. They were willing to help Jack with his contact with God and his knowledge of his will and the power to carry out that will.

Jack's doubts fell away and a strong, solid faith took their place. The support of those men who had struggled where he had struggled, along with practicing Step Eleven, helped Jack stop relapsing. It also helped him connect better with his wife, who had offered Jack grace. Jack did the work, and he allowed God to do some work also. In the end, Jack felt better connected to those men, his wife, and God. Those connections freed him to speak truth if he was troubled or tempted and find help. And he grew closer to the loving God he was coming to understand in new and richer ways daily.

STEP ELEVEN

We sought through prayer and meditation to improve our conscious contact with God, praying only for knowledge of his will for us and the power to carry it out.

Step Eleven is the next maintenance step, in which we practice a new way of living. In the first three steps, we commit ourselves to turn away from addictive behaviors and thinking.

Steps Four through Nine help us to clean out the past, and now we can focus on the present. Step Eleven gives us our spiritual marching orders as we seek through "prayer and meditation to improve our conscious contact with God."

We simplify our prayer life by praying "only for the knowledge of his will for us and the power to carry that out." King David's song of praise in 2 Samuel 22 shares with us the specifics of David's conscious contact with God. God in his many attributes is active on behalf of his people, even a single person such as David or ourselves.

What started in Step Three with surrendering our lives is now expanded in Step Eleven. We seek the will of God in our lives on a more earnest level. We also request the power that we need to carry that out, beginning with staying sober or clean from our addiction. Our substance, behavioral, or emotional addiction cannot satisfy our spiritual hunger—we have proven that. We must now find a connection to God that goes beyond mere belief—it must be a relationship.

Step Eleven guides us to seek God for who he is more than for what he can give us. We have experienced God's grace and mercy, which ignited our recovery. Without God's continuing to act in our lives, however, we are left with our own unsteady heart, mind, and behavior. For long-term recovery, we must have God's power and help.

Using prayer and meditation as tools, we actively and continually seek conscious contact with God. An example of this type of prayer and meditation is found in Psalm 27. It reveals how God works in our lives; how through praise and trust, we can live in serenity. When we grasp that God sees each person as important and valuable, we can trust that our well-being is in his care.

Because God cares about us and loves us in wondrous ways, Step Eleven builds the foundation of our present recovery on our relationship with God. In Psalm 65:1-4, David points us to joy in this relationship as we realize that we are welcome in

God's presence. Working Step Eleven makes this a daily practice. Prayer and meditation are the vehicles for attaining conscious contact. Prayer is speaking directly to God, and meditation is humbly and expectantly listening to him.

Step Eleven is focused on the present, which is different from the steps that deal with the past and with introspection. After all the inventories of our past in addiction, in which we realize that we have missed the mark on God's will, this step leads us to seek God's will for us today. We grow in humility as we ask for knowledge of his will and acknowledge that the power to carry it out also comes from God. As we exchange our old lives and objectives for his new ones every day, we are establishing a new pattern of living by faith. The former pattern meant keeping secrets that kept us sick, but Psalm 119 offers us the secret that strengthens and heals us, which is God's Word hidden in our hearts. The secrets of old behaviors in addiction will bring destruction and death, but when we hide God's Word in our hearts, we gain the ability to avoid addiction and sin against God. This must be a daily activity because each new day is filled with possibilities and temptations. Today, we choose the path of Step Eleven in meditation and prayer to recover daily and deepen our relationship with God.

One huge challenge of Step Eleven for anyone with tendencies toward addiction, dependency, or relapsing back into them is learning to wait on God. Isaiah 40:31 says, "But those who trust in the LORD will find new strength. They will soar high on wings like eagles. They will run and not grow weary. They will walk and not faint." Impatience is a mark of most everyone who struggles and lives for the immediate fix, high, or relief that comes from a sexual encounter or any sexual experience. Now, we must learn to wait upon the Lord if we want to find new strength for recovery. We may even become impatient with our progress, but when we are in recovery for the long haul, Step Eleven directs us to depend more and more upon God. The result is the ability to turn less and less to addiction for relief, comfort, and joy.

Though Step Eleven presents a simple approach to prayer

and meditation, it is often difficult. Sometimes we resist because we fear that his will may be contrary to our own. This is when we must reach again for the humility to align our will with God's will, knowing that his light will keep us from the darkness of addiction and relapse. This spiritual step expands our tolerance of his light and gives us a previously unknown measure of freedom.

QUESTIONS FOR **STEP ELEVEN**

A New Hiding Place *2 Samuel 22:1-33*

1. How was addiction a hiding place from life for me? Compare this with having God as a hiding place.

_____

_____

_____

2. Describe how I experience "conscious contact" with God:

_____

_____

_____

Thirst for God *Psalm 27:1-6*

1. What do I most seek from God?

_____

_____

_____

2. What is difficult about trusting God with my requests?

_____

_____

_____

Joy in God's Presence _Psalm 65:1-4_

1. Is there anything that keeps me from accepting God's forgiveness?

_____

_____

_____

2. What scares me about the knowledge of God's will for me?

_____

_____

_____

Finding God _Psalm 105:1-9_

1. Is my life changing daily? Am I noticing when I am resentful, selfish, dishonest, or afraid today? Identify ways that I am changing:

_____

_____

_____

2. Am I aware of others' feelings, needs, and rights? What have I noticed today? If I am lacking in this, why?

_____

_____

_____

Powerful Secrets *Psalm 119:1-11*

1. What am I hiding in my heart—secrets of old behaviors and issues, or God's Word? After close examination, what is really in there?

_____

_____

_____

2. List what I can thank God for today:

_____

_____

_____

Patient Waiting *Isaiah 40:28-31*

1. How does impatience show itself in my attitude and behaviors?

_____

_____

_____

2. Am I impatient about my progress in recovery? Do I expect myself to "get it" the first time? Do I expect perfection?

_____

_____

_____

3. Why is it hard to "trust in the Lord"?

_____

_____

_____

Friends of the Light *John 3:18-21*

1. In what areas of my life am I still afraid to seek God's will?

_____

_____

_____

2. When I think that I am hearing God's will, whose power do I act on? Am I tempted to do God's will in my own power?

_____

_____

_____

God wants us in a vibrant, growing, and intimate relationship with him. In the first ten steps, we were working to strip away and throw off anything that stood in the way of our walking closer to the path God has chosen for us. Now we must stop walking long enough to allow God's presence so profoundly into our lives that we walk in his will and totally under his power.

Prayer for Step Eleven

Dear God,
Thank you for showing me the path that leads to you. Thank you for being with me throughout this journey and for being with me now. Allow me to experience you in new and intimate ways. As I meditate on your Word, expand its meaning and deepen my knowledge of who you are and what you want for my life. When I am afraid, give me courage. When I am weak, give me your strength. And when I am distracted, give me clarity of purpose and the desire to carry out your will.
Amen.

PROFILE

We (Steve and Dave) have been working together, writing together, and sharing friendship for almost forty years. Through that time, we have both dealt with issues that benefited from us understanding, working, and living into the Twelve Steps of Life Recovery. We have had our fair share of issues and addictions, and working the Twelve Steps has affected our lives for the better. We shared each struggle and did what we could to support each other. Our spiritual awakenings occurred many years before we met, but since then, both of us have continued to wake up to new insights from God's truth that apply to recovery and our relationship together.

We are still together doing what we love to do best. We write together, we are on New Life Live radio together, and we still speak together about recovery. We are continuing to develop new ways for people to access Life Recovery materials, such as the Life Recovery app. We are still creating new organizations that we hope will be around for years to come, such as the International Christian Coaching Institute and the Life Recovery Institute at Indiana Wesleyan University. Neither of us is relaxing in a hammock during the day because we have work to do.

In any partnership where new things are being developed, there is opportunity for misunderstanding, conflict, and resentment. Over the past forty years, we have watched many other partnerships like ours handle their disputes poorly and eventually go their separate ways. In many cases the split was handled so poorly that it made the Christian faith look bad. We are often asked why we think we are still working together when so few other former partners can even tolerate each other.

We tell them we think it is because of the biblical foundations of Step Twelve. We try "to practice these principles in all our affairs." That means we stay current with each other, and we don't drag past conflicts or issues into today. We tell each other if we are bothered by something, and we let it go. We work with a spirit of forgiveness and grace for each other. We hold each other accountable. Each is responsible for a different area in our work and we expect the other to do it, but we offer grace when it does not get done on time. Neither of us is close to perfect, and both of us become frustrated with each other. But our love and respect for each other override everything else, and very quickly today's problem becomes a faint memory in the past rather than a destructive wedge in the future. To do that we have to practice these powerful principles in all our affairs.

We also have a common bond that keeps us working together. We want to carry this message to as many people as possible. We want to do what we can do while we are alive so that as many people as possible can benefit from the Twelve Steps and the groups that meet to use them. Whether it is a prisoner serving a life sentence attending a Life Recovery Step Study or a wealthy executive on a private jet opening up *The Life Recovery Bible* for a morning devotional, we are grateful that God has allowed us to carry this message to them. And we both continue to carry the message to others in our churches and the individuals God sends our way.

This is our profile: two fellow strugglers who are struggling to practice these principles with each other and with those around us, while we work together to carry the message to as many people as possible. We are two men who have been where you are and who want to encourage you to stay healthy and hopeful by staying connected to others with honesty and humility and never stop working the Twelve Steps. They really do work if you work them.

STEP TWELVE

Having had a spiritual awakening as a result of these steps, we tried to carry this message to others, and to practice these principles in all our affairs.

There are three parts to Step Twelve: the affirmation of our spiritual awakening, carrying the message of that awakening, and practicing these principles in our entire life.

By working diligently on the first eleven steps, we have acquired a healthier view of ourselves, others, and God. This has enabled us to live free of the bondage of our sexual addiction and the shame of our past behaviors on a more consistent and contented basis. Even if we previously believed in God, we have achieved a greater level of surrender, humility, and serenity than we ever imagined. Allowing the Lord Jesus to free us from the burden and compulsion of addiction takes a measure of faith and humility that is challenging even to experienced Christians. The obsession with sex and the compulsive behaviors have painfully exposed our human limitations, frailties, and absolute inability to save ourselves. The addicted self has only one focus: the next person or porn or anything that provides a moment of relief. Recovery through the first eleven steps teaches us to surrender that self-centered will and bring it into line with God's will, which yields freedom from captivity.

Now we embark on working the second part of Step Twelve: carrying the message. After living in the spiritual poverty of addiction and dependency, recovering sex addicts of all types are able to live a full life in relationship with God and others. This good news is too wonderful to keep hidden. "No one lights a lamp and then puts it under a basket. Instead, a lamp is placed on a stand, where it gives light to everyone in the house," says Jesus in Matthew 5:15. An amazing expansion of our maturity in recovery occurs as we share our experience, strength, and hope with others. We keep it alive in us as we share compassionately with fellow strugglers. It becomes our spiritual mission to share the message of recovery and liberation with captive addicts.

Since we have been freed from the tyranny of addiction by working the Twelve Steps, we have a new outlook on life and a deeper connection with God's Spirit. Working Step Twelve means that we must be ready to share with anyone at any moment about recovery from anything. If our primary problem is sexual addiction, we are not limited to helping others who have struggled with sex. These steps are for anyone going through anything because they are based on the Bible. Working through the steps provides us with a foundational wisdom that others who are willing to surrender will come to appreciate. We have no need to feel limited in God's ability to use it beyond our primary struggle.

Helping another person requires two things from us. First, we must tell our story to another person about what we were like in our addiction, what happened to convince us to seek recovery, and what we are like now that we are released from addiction by working the Twelve Steps. Doing this is helping us win the credibility battle with the other person so they can have some confidence we really do know where they have been and what would be helpful to them. At the same time, we are reminding ourselves of the path we have traveled, keeping denial from creeping into our thoughts and leading us to relapse. Second, we are required to be humble. Our humility and compassion develop as we share. Admitting to another that we are recovering from an addiction, especially sexual addiction, takes humility and the courage to risk being rebuffed, yet we know where the other is, emotionally and spiritually. Our sharing can be of powerful help to others. Taking on this responsibility to carry the message brings a measure of maturity.

The third part of Step Twelve is practicing these principles in all our affairs. Practicing these principles involves the continual application of all twelve steps to our life circumstances. Let's review the principles we have been experiencing through working the Twelve Steps:

STEP ONE: *We must recognize our powerlessness in the unmanageability of our lives daily.*

STEP TWO: *God removes our insanity and restores our wholeness.*

STEP THREE: *We surrender to God and let go of control.*

STEPS FOUR AND FIVE: *We make an honest inventory of ourselves (not others) and share our confession with another person.*

STEPS SIX AND SEVEN: *In humility, we seek help from God to cleanse us and fill us with new strengths.*

STEPS EIGHT AND NINE: *We recognize the harm we have caused to others and take action to heal our damaged relationships.*

STEP TEN: *We continue to take inventory of our behavior, and when we are wrong, we promptly admit it.*

STEP ELEVEN: *We are increasingly more conscious of God's presence.*

STEP TWELVE: *We give away what we have gained in our journey through the steps and remain in recovery in every life situation.*

Remaining in recovery is similar to what Jesus said to his disciples in John 15:5: "Those who remain in me, and I in them, will produce much fruit. For apart from me you can do nothing." We cannot practice these principles of the Twelve Steps without being connected to him, so our priority is to apply these steps in any problem, event, situation, job, or relationship—in other words, through anything that life throws at us. When we connect to Jesus by deepening our conscious contact, he enables us to live more effectively, responsibly, and joyously.

As we maintain our sobriety and persist in recovery by working the Twelve Steps, we find benefits that were not obtainable before. In the midst of addictive behaviors and substances, our lives may have seemed to wander meaninglessly, but now they are filled with purpose and direction. We learn that we can be content with the conditions set before us. We learn that we can accept and handle tragedy and stress with serenity and courage. We learn to appropriately connect to our loved ones and seek to live well with everyone we encounter, meeting them with compassion, grace, and acceptance. We learn that our relationship with God is the key to all of these tremendous gifts of recovery, and that an "attitude of gratitude" is the salve for any irritability or other emotional disturbance. We begin to see that the basis of life is partnership with God and people.

Our shortsighted purposes for our lives begin to fade as we realize that with God's help, we can conquer our fatal addictions and suffocating empty dependencies. The miracle of this partnership with God is so awe-inspiring that we are encouraged to continue recovery no matter how arduous it may be. We realize that material worldly success pales in comparison to living vitally and purposefully and carrying out what God wants for us and from us, as found in God's Word: "O people, the LORD has told you what is good, and this is what he requires of you: to do what is right, to love mercy, and to walk humbly with your God" (Micah 6:8).

QUESTIONS FOR **STEP TWELVE**

Our Mission *Isaiah 61:1-3*

1. How have I passed through the pain and despair of enslavement to sexual obsessions and compulsions, and moved into healing and freedom?

_____

_____

_____

2. Having had a "spiritual awakening" after being set free from my addiction, am I excited, willing, or hesitant to share my experience, strength, and hope with others who are struggling with addiction? Why?

_____

_____

_____

Our Story *Mark 16:14-18*

Describe the story of your spiritual awakening and how the first eleven steps have brought spiritual principles, truths, and healing into your life. Describe what you were like, what happened, and what you are like now.

_____

_____

_____

_____

_____

_____

_____

_____

Sharing Together *John 15:5-15*

1. Am I connected to the vine? How do the Twelve Steps help me to "remain" in him?

_____

_____

_____

2. Is my recovery attractive to other strugglers because I am becoming more loving rather than condemning those who need my help?

_____

_____

_____

3. What am I doing to reach out with Jesus' love?

_____

_____

_____

Listening First _Acts 8:26-40_

1. What is my attitude about sharing my story of recovery: Am I reluctant to tell my story, or am I the type who wants to share too much, too soon, with too many people?

_____

_____

_____

2. From either extreme, am I willing to wait for God's timing for sharing recovery?

_____

_____

_____

3. Do I see my story as valuable to God's plan? Describe how.

_____

_____

_____

Seeing Your Progress *1 Timothy 4:14-16*

1. Paul encourages Timothy to "throw yourself into your tasks so that everyone will see your progress." What changes in my life can others observe since I have been sober and working the Twelve Steps?

_____

_____

_____

2. Paul wanted Timothy not only to teach others, but to be an example. When I share my story with others, am I preaching or sharing my experience, strength, and hope?

_____

_____

_____

3. Am I able to let the other person make his or her own decision by relinquishing control and letting God do his work?

_____

_____

_____

Never Forget *Titus 3:1-5*

What do I remember about the last time I messed up or acted out? Describe that time, including actions, feelings, behaviors, and thoughts that led up to it and followed it:

_____

_____

_____

The Narrow Road *1 Peter 4:1-4*

1. Peter points out: "You have had enough in the past of the evil things that godless people enjoy—their immorality and lust, their feasting and drunkenness and wild parties" (1 Peter 4:3). What was so painful about my addiction that I became willing to suffer for Christ (1 Peter 4:1-2) the pains of recovery?

   _____

   _____

   _____

2. Does the approval or judgment of others keep me from sharing recovery? Do I fear negative rumors?

   _____

   _____

   _____

3. How can I work the Twelve Steps on this fear?

   _____

   _____

   _____

CONCLUDING THOUGHTS

Our temptation now is to think that we have finished the Twelve Steps. The reality is that the steps are never really done because we never quit growing emotionally or spiritually. By practicing the Twelve Steps, we have a path for life and a connection with God that yields greater humility and reverence for his grace and power.

You never have to wonder how to carry this message of transformation to others. It happens when you integrate the Twelve Step principles into every area of your life. You don't have to loudly proclaim the message; your changed life speaks for itself. Attending weekly meetings and working the steps are only meaningful if they result in a remarkable life that is noticeably different than before—without the same destructive habits and patterns. The message is carried further and better by a kind tongue than by articulate lips. So, carry the message of hope and transformation as you love others with all you have and all you are.

We conclude with this blessing and encouragement from Peter:

> May God give you more and more grace and peace as you grow in your knowledge of God and Jesus our Lord. By his divine power, God has given us everything we need for living a godly life. We have received all of this by coming to know him, the one who called us to himself by means of his marvelous glory and excellence. And because of his glory and excellence, he has given us great and precious promises. These are the promises that enable you to share his divine nature

and escape the world's corruption caused by human desires. In view of all this, make every effort to respond to God's promises. Supplement your faith with a generous provision of moral excellence, and moral excellence with knowledge, and knowledge with self-control, and self-control with patient endurance, and patient endurance with godliness, and godliness with brotherly affection, and brotherly affection with love for everyone. (2 Peter 1:2-7)

Prayer for Recovery

Dear Lord,
Help me focus my will today on my eagerness to do your will, through working the Twelve Steps and practicing these principles in all that I do, and not to chase evil desires that would stir up my addiction. Amen.

SCRIPTURE INDEX